Dorothy Sleightholme's
FARMHOUSE RECIPES

Dorothy Sleightholme's

FARMHOUSE
RECIPES

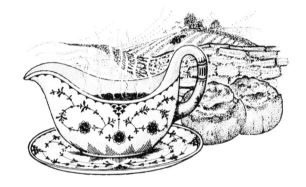

Hamlyn
London · New York · Sydney · Toronto

*The paintings and watercolours reproduced
in the book were kindly lent by
Anthony Dallas & Sons Ltd.
9 Old Bond Street, London W1
Telephone 01-491-8662
Specialists in landscape paintings*

Published in 1983 by
The Hamlyn Publishing Group Limited
London · New York · Sydney · Toronto
Astronaut House, Feltham, Middlesex, England
© Copyright The Hamlyn Publishing Group Limited 1983

ISBN 0 600 32337 4

Front cover photograph by James Jackson
Author's photograph by Peter Harris
Photography by David Johnson

Filmset in 10 on 11¼ Monophoto Goudy by
Tameside Filmsetting Limited
Ashton-under-Lyne, Lancashire, England

Printed in Italy

Contents

Useful Facts and Figures

Notes on metrication

In this book quantities are given in metric and Imperial measures. Exact conversion from Imperial to metric measures does not usually give very convenient working quantities and so the metric measures have been rounded off into units of 25 grams. The table below shows the recommended equivalents.

Ounces	Approx g to nearest whole figure	Recommended conversion to nearest unit of 25	Ounces	Approx g to nearest whole figure	Recommended conversion to nearest unit of 25
1	28	25	11	312	300
2	57	50	12	340	350
3	85	75	13	368	375
4	113	100	14	396	400
5	142	150	15	425	425
6	170	175	16 (1 lb)	454	450
7	198	200	17	482	475
8	227	225	18	510	500
9	255	250	19	539	550
10	283	275	20 (1¼ lb)	567	575

Note: When converting quantities over 20 oz first add the appropriate figures in the centre column, then adjust to the nearest unit of 25. As a general guide, 1 kg (1000 g) equals 2.2 lb or about 2 lb 3 oz. This method of conversion gives good results in nearly all cases, although in certain pastry and cake recipes a more accurate conversion is necessary to produce a balanced recipe.

Liquid measures The millilitre has been used in this book and the following table gives a few examples.

Imperial	Approx ml to nearest whole figure	Recommended ml
¼ pint	142	150 ml
½ pint	283	300 ml
¾ pint	425	450 ml
1 pint	567	600 ml
1½ pints	851	1000 ml (1 litre)

Spoon measures All spoon measures given in this book are level unless otherwise stated.

Can sizes At present, cans are marked with the exact (usually to the nearest whole number) metric equivalent of the Imperial weight of the contents, so we have followed this practice when giving can sizes.

Oven temperatures
The table below gives recommended equivalents.

	°C	°F	Gas Mark
Very cool	110	225	$\frac{1}{4}$
	120	250	$\frac{1}{2}$
Cool	140	275	1
	150	300	2
Moderate	160	325	3
	180	350	4
Moderately hot	190	375	5
	200	400	6
Hot	220	425	7
	230	450	8
Very hot	240	475	9

Notes for American and Australian users

In America the 8-oz measuring cup is used. In Australia metric measures are now used in conjunction with the standard 250 ml measuring cup. The Imperial pint, used in Britain and Australia, is 20 fl oz, while the American tablespoon differs from both the British and American tablespoons; the table below gives a comparison. The British standard tablespoon, which has been used throughout this book, holds 17.7 ml, the American 14.2 ml, and the Australian 20 ml. A teaspoon holds approximately 5 ml in all three countries.

British	American	Australian
1 teaspoon	1 teaspoon	1 teaspoon
1 tablespoon	1 tablespoon	1 tablespoon
2 tablespoons	3 tablespoons	2 tablespoons
$3\frac{1}{2}$ tablespoons	4 tablespoons	3 tablespoons
4 tablespoons	5 tablespoons	$3\frac{1}{2}$ tablespoons

An Imperial/American guide to solid and liquid measures

Imperial	American	Imperial	American
Solid measures		**Liquid measures**	
1 lb butter or		$\frac{1}{4}$ pint liquid	$\frac{2}{3}$ cup liquid
margarine	2 cups	$\frac{1}{2}$ pint	$1\frac{1}{4}$ cups
4 cups	$\frac{1}{4}$ pint	2 cups	1 lb flour
1 lb granulated		1 pint	$2\frac{1}{2}$ cups
or castor sugar	2 cups	$1\frac{1}{2}$ pints	$3\frac{3}{4}$ cups
1 lb icing sugar	3 cups	2 pints	5 cups ($2\frac{1}{2}$
8 oz rice	1 cup		pints)

Note: When making any of the recipes in this book, only follow one set of measures as they are not interchangeable.

Introduction

Over the years I have collected, tried and enjoyed thousands of recipes, adapting most of them to my own ideas and tastes. Of these there is a whole treasury of ones that have gone down well time and time again in my home, whether they are old favourites we all know and love or new recipes which widen the range of traditional home cooking, and I have had a lot of pleasure out of putting them together in a book.

I hope that this collection of soups, both light and filling, traditional roasts and casseroles, simple but tasty bakes and supper dishes and deliciously tempting puddings, pastries and cakes will have something to offer you and that you won't be afraid to alter and adapt the recipes to your liking as you use them. For good cooks are not born, they become good through time, patience, experience, enjoyment of what they are doing – and perhaps with the help of a little forbearance from their family and friends.

Dorothy Sleightholme

Basic Recipes

Stock

You can make a good stock from almost any kind of bones and meat trimmings, although the most usual ones to use are chicken and veal for a light stock and beef for a dark one. Lamb bones make a delicious, rich stock for a winter vegetable soup, while the water left over from boiling a ham or bacon joint should never be thrown away; on its own it provides a wonderful stock for making lentil or split pea soup.

Here is a basic recipe for stock which you can adapt according to what bones you want to use:

675 g/1½ lb chicken, beef, veal or lamb bones and meat
trimmings
1.15–1.75 litres/2–3 pints water
1 onion, sliced
bouquet garni (parsley, thyme, bay leaf, sage)
generous pinch of salt

Put all the ingredients together into a pan, cover and bring to the boil. Simmer over a low heat for 2–3 hours, skimming from time to time the scum that rises to the surface.

Strain the stock into a bowl, allow to cool and chill it in the refrigerator so that any fat can solidfy on the top. Remove this and use the stock as required, adding water or boiling it further to reduce it, according to taste.

Note Do not add much salt to the stock while it is cooking. You may have to reduce the liquid considerably later and you do not want it to end up being too salty.

When making chicken stock, use the giblets as well, unless you particularly want a light stock. The giblets will add flavour but will also tend to darken the stock.

White Sauce

25 g/1 oz butter or margarine
25 g/1 oz plain flour
150–450 ml/¼–¾ pint milk
salt and pepper

Melt the fat in a pan, stir in the flour and cook for 1 minute. Gradually pour in enough milk to give the sauce the consistency you require: 150 ml/¼ pint will make a thick, binding sauce, suitable for soufflés, flan fillings and croquettes; 300 ml/½ pint will give a coating sauce, just right for a fish pie or a macaroni cheese; while 450 ml/¾ pint will give the sauce a pouring consistency. Keep stirring as you pour in the milk and bring the sauce to the boil, then allow it to boil for 2 minutes, still stirring. Season it to taste with salt and pepper and use as required, or follow the variations given below.

Variations

Cheese Sauce Add a teaspoon of made mustard to the basic white sauce above, and stir in about 75 g/3 oz strong grated cheese. Beat well to melt the cheese. Serve with grilled or fried fish, chicken or vegetables.
Parsley Sauce Add 2–3 tablespoons chopped parsley to the basic white sauce (the sauce should be quite green). Excellent with ham and white fish.
Onion Sauce Boil 2 or 3 sliced onions in a little water until tender. Drain, then blend to a purée and add to the basic white sauce, seasoning as necessary. Keep the cooking liquor for gravy or soups.
　Serve with lamb, rabbit or boiled tripe.
Vanilla Sauce Omit the salt and pepper and stir in 1 tablespoon sugar and ½–1 teaspoon vanilla essence to taste.
Lemon Sauce Omit the salt and pepper and add 1 tablespoon sugar and finely grated rind of a lemon.
Mocha Sauce Omit the salt and pepper and stir in 1 tablespoon sugar, 25 g/1 oz plain dessert chocolate, grated, and 2 teaspoons coffee essence.

Horseradish Sauce

2–3 tablespoons grated horseradish or a
proprietary horseradish cream
100 ml/4 fl oz double cream
salt
juice of ½ lemon

Lightly whip the cream and stir in the horseradish to taste,
and the flavourings. Horseradish sauce is the perfect English
accompaniment to roast beef (page 38), but don't forget that it
also goes well with fish.

Bread Sauce

1 small onion
2 cloves
300 ml/½ pint milk
pinch of salt
6 peppercorns
small piece of bay leaf
50 g/2 oz fresh white breadcrumbs
15 g/½ oz butter

Skin the onion, cut it in half and stick a clove in each piece.
Put into a saucepan with the milk, salt, peppercorns, and bay
leaf. Cover, bring to simmering point, then take off the heat.
Leave to infuse for about 20 minutes, then strain it.

Put the breadcrumbs in a small ovenproof dish, pour on
the strained milk, dot the butter on top, and place on a low
shelf in the oven. Bread sauce can be cooked at the same time
as the poultry with which it is usually served, and can sit in
the oven for 30 or 40 minutes. Otherwise, if the oven is not
being used: after straining the milk, pour it back into a
saucepan, add the crumbs and butter, and simmer for 5–6
minutes, stirring from time to time.

Apple Sauce

450 g/1 lb cooking apples
2–3 tablespoons water
15 g/½ oz butter
grated rind of ½ lemon
sugar to taste

Peel, core and slice the apples and simmer them in the water until quite tender. Purée in the blender, or push through a sieve. Add the butter and lemon rind, and sugar to taste.

Gooseberry Sauce

Make as for Apple Sauce, substituting the same weight of topped and tailed gooseberries, and serve with grilled mackerel (page 26).

Mint Sauce

bunch of mint
2 tablespoons sugar
2 tablespoons boiling water
3 tablespoons vinegar, or to taste

Chop the mint finely with the sugar, and place in a small bowl. Add the boiling water, and stir until the sugar is dissolved. Add vinegar to taste. Allow to stand for about 30 minutes, then pour into a sauceboat, and serve with lamb.

Soups and Starters

Nothing can be more welcoming on a cold, frosty day than the sight of a large saucepan bubbling away on the hob, filled with delicious, piping hot soup. The secret of most good soups is the stock, whether you are using a light chicken or veal one for a cream soup or a dark beef stock for a chunky vegetable soup. But anything you can add to the stock will make a special difference – a handful of celery leaves, a few parsley stalks, some bacon bits, a little chutney or honey left in the bottom of the jar – all these will enrich the stock to give that unique, nourishing flavour of real home-made soup.

If you don't want to serve a soup, a simple pâté or a mousse may be the answer. Easy to prepare and serve, the starters I have given here tend to vanish in next to no time from my table! Some of them, like Ham and Cheese Croquettes, will double up as savouries and can be served as special tea-time snacks.

Scotch Broth

*There's eating and drinking in this soup, as they say. A real
brew for northerners, perfect for keeping out their winter cold. Scotch
Broth makes a complete meal in itself.*

450 g/1 lb scrag end of mutton
1.75 litres/3 pints water
50 g/2 oz pearl barley
1 carrot
1 small turnip
2 leeks
1 or 2 sticks of celery
1 large onion
salt and pepper
chopped parsley for garnish

Cut away any fat from the mutton, and joint it. Place it in a
large pan with the water. Wash the barley and add to the pan.
Bring to a boil and simmer for 1 hour.

Strain the broth, discarding the bones and returning the
meat and barley to the liquid in the pan. Next prepare the
vegetables. Cut the carrot, turnip and celery into dice, slice
the leeks and add them all to the pan. Simmer, with the lid on,
until the ingredients are tender. Season with salt and pepper,
and serve sprinkled with parsley. SERVES 6–8.

Oxtail Soup

1 oxtail
50 g/2 oz dripping
1 small turnip, peeled and cut into dice
1 large carrot, sliced
2.25 litres/4 pints beef stock
¼ teaspoon celery salt
bouquet garni, consisting of sprigs of thyme, parsley, bay
leaf and 6–8 peppercorns tied in muslin
pinch each of powdered mace and cloves
25 g/1 oz flour
a little gravy browning

If it isn't already prepared, ask your butcher to cut the oxtail into sections, then blanch it by pouring over boiling water: leave for 1 or 2 minutes, then dry on kitchen paper.

Melt the dripping in a large pan, and fry the oxtail with the prepared vegetables, until brown. Add the stock, celery salt, bouquet garni, cloves and mace. Cover and simmer gently for about 3 hours until tender.

Strain the soup and thicken it with the flour mixed to a paste with a little water, adding a little gravy browning if necessary.

The larger pieces of oxtail can be served as a main course with vegetables, the meat from the smaller pieces can be added to the soup. Oxtail Soup is better made the day before it is needed, allowed to stand, and then the excess fat skimmed off the top. SERVES 6–8.

Cauliflower Soup

1 medium cauliflower
1 onion or 2–3 shallots
300 ml/$\frac{1}{2}$ pint milk
2 teaspoons cornflour
450 ml/$\frac{3}{4}$ pint chicken or ham stock (page 9)
$\frac{1}{4}$ teaspoon mace
2 tablespoons single cream
salt and pepper
chopped fresh parsley or a sprinkling of paprika to garnish

Cut away the leaves and hard stalk from the cauliflower and break the cauliflower into small florets. Finely chop the onion or shallots. Cook the vegetables in a little boiling salted water for about 15 minutes, until tender, then pass them through a sieve with their cooking water or blend them to a purée in a liquidiser. Add a little milk if the purée is too stiff.

Whisk the cornflour into a little more of the milk and put the mixture into a pan with the stock, the vegetable purée and any remaining milk. Bring the soup to the boil, stirring from time to time. Take the pan off the heat and add the mace, cream and salt and pepper to taste – you may not need to add any salt at all if you are using ham stock.

Pour the soup into four individual bowls and sprinkle each with a little chopped fresh parsley or paprika to garnish. SERVES 4–6.

Lentil Soup

Illustrated on page 33

225 g/8 oz lentils
1 medium onion or 2–3 shallots
1 carrot
2 sticks celery
600 ml/1 pint bacon or ham stock (page 9)
150 ml/¼ pint milk
salt and black pepper
25 g/1 oz butter
chopped celery leaves for garnish

Wash and drain the lentils, put them in a bowl with plenty of water and leave them to soak overnight. Drain, transfer them to a pan with just enough fresh water to cover, bring to the boil, cover the pan and simmer the lentils for 40 minutes – 1 hour, until tender. Add more water during cooking if necessary.

Finely slice the onion or shallots. Trim and chop the carrot and celery, reserving the celery leaves on one side. Put the vegetables in the pan followed by half the stock, bring the soup once more to the boil and simmer it for about 15 minutes, until the vegetables are tender. Now take the pan off the heat, if you want a smooth soup, and pass the contents through a sieve or blend them to a purée in a liquidiser. Pour the soup into a clean pan and add the remaining stock, together with the milk. Season to taste; if the stock was fairly salty to begin with, you will only need to add a little pepper.

Return the soup to the boil, stirring occasionally, and add the butter. Finely chop the reserved celery leaves. Divide the soup between four individual bowls and sprinkle a few chopped celery leaves on top of each. SERVES 4.

French Onion Soup

675 g/1½ lb onions
1 clove garlic
25 g/1 oz butter
1 teaspoon sugar
1 teaspoon plain flour
900 ml–1.15 litres/1½–2 pints beef stock (page 9)
salt and pepper
4 thick slices French bread
100 g/4 oz grated Cheddar or Gruyère cheese

Slice the onions into fine rings. Peel and crush the garlic clove. Melt the butter in a pan and fry the onion and garlic gently for about 10 minutes, stirring from time to time.

Add the sugar, cover the pan and continue cooking, stirring occasionally, until the onions are tender and golden. Sprinkle in the flour to absorb any remaining fat in the pan and cook for 1 minute, stirring. Pour in 900 ml/1½ pints of the stock, cover the pan, bring the soup to the boil and simmer it for 20 minutes. Add the remaining stock if you think it needs it. Season to taste with salt and pepper.

Lightly toast one side of the pieces of bread under a low grill and sprinkle the other side with the grated cheese. Place the toast under the grill until the cheese melts.

Transfer the soup to four individual bowls, float a slice of toasted bread and cheese on top of each and serve. SERVES 4.

Mulligatawny Soup

2 large carrots
2 sticks celery
2 large onions
1 large cooking apple
40 g/1½ oz dripping or margarine
1 tablespoon plain flour
3 teaspoons curry powder
900 ml/1½ pints well-flavoured stock made from lamb bones
or from scrag end of neck of lamb (page 9)
salt and pepper

Trim the carrots and celery and finely slice them, together with the onions. Quarter, core and finely chop the apple. Melt the fat in a large pan, add the chopped vegetables and apple and soften them gently for about 10 minutes. Do not allow them to brown.

Stir in the flour and curry powder and continue cooking for 1 minute. Pour in the stock, bring the soup to the boil, stirring continuously, and simmer it for 15–20 minutes. Season it with salt and pepper to taste and serve. SERVES 4–6.

Chilled Watercress Soup

1 large bunch of watercress
175 g/6 oz potatoes
1 large onion or 3–4 shallots
1 clove garlic
25 g/1 oz butter
600 ml/1 pint chicken stock (page 9)
small bay leaf
$\frac{3}{4}$ teaspoon salt
$\frac{1}{4}$ teaspoon pepper
3 tablespoons single cream
grated nutmeg to garnish

Wash the watercress, discarding any thick stalks and yellow leaves and allow it to drain.

Peel and slice the potatoes. Chop the onion or shallots. Peel and crush the garlic. Melt the butter in a pan, add the chopped vegetables and garlic and sauté them gently until soft but not coloured. Pour in the stock and add the watercress, bay leaf, salt and pepper. Bring the soup to the boil, cover the pan and simmer for 20–25 minutes, until all the vegetables are soft. Remove the bay leaf, allow the soup to cool and pass it through a sieve or blend it to a purée in a liquidiser. Chill the soup in the refrigerator.

Before serving, taste and adjust the seasoning. Pour the soup into four individual bowls, stir a little cream into each and sprinkle nutmeg on top. SERVES 4.

Kipper Pâté

2 large kippers
75 g/3 oz butter, softened
1 tablespoon lemon juice
1–2 tablespoons double cream
pinch of cayenne or a generous grinding of black pepper
¼ teaspoon mace

Soak excess salt out of the kippers first by placing them in a large bowl and covering them with boiling water. Leave them to stand for 10 minutes, then drain and remove the skin and bones from the fish. Mash the kippers and work in the butter, lemon juice and enough cream to give the pâté a smooth, not too dry texture. Beat well and season it with the cayenne or pepper and the mace. SERVES 4.

Chicken Liver Pâté

225 g/8 oz chicken livers
50 g/2 oz streaky bacon
1 small onion
50 g/2 oz butter
1–2 tablespoons double cream
salt and black pepper
¼ teaspoon mace
pinch of dried mixed herbs (optional)

Wash and trim the chicken livers and cut them into small pieces. Remove the rind from the bacon and finely chop the rashers, together with the onion. Melt the butter in a pan and sauté the bacon and onion gently for 5–7 minutes, until cooked. Add the chicken livers and continue frying for 3 minutes or until the liver, too, is cooked.

Blend the mixture to a purée, adding just enough cream to moisten it. Season the pâté with salt and pepper to taste and stir in the mace and the herbs, if used. Pour it into a lightly buttered dish and chill it in the refrigerator. SERVES 4.

Salmon Mousse

Illustrated on page 33

1 (225-g/8-oz) can salmon
2 teaspoons tomato purée
2 tablespoons water
1 tablespoon wine vinegar
15 g/½ oz powdered gelatine
1 (170-g/6-oz) can evaporated milk *or* 150 ml/¼ pint whipping
cream
1 teaspoon lemon juice
1 egg white
salt and white pepper to taste
Garnish
1 stuffed olive
2 gherkins
slices of lemon and cucumber if wished

Drain the salmon and flake it, removing any bones and skin. Mash the fish with the tomato purée. Pour the water and vinegar into a bowl held over a pan of hot water. Sprinkle the gelatine into the bowl and whisk until it has dissolved. Beat the evaporated milk until thick, adding the lemon juice little by little as it thickens; or, whip the cream lightly, in this case omitting the lemon juice. Whisk the egg white until stiff.

Stir the gelatine mixture into the salmon, season to taste and gently fold in the milk followed by the egg white. Rinse out an oval 600-ml/1-pint mould with cold water, pour in the salmon mixture and leave the mousse to set in the refrigerator for 3–4 hours.

Dip the mould into cold water and turn the mousse out on to a serving dish. Cut the stuffed olive in half. Drain the gherkins and make four or five cuts down the length of each, slicing only to half-way. Spread out the slices to make a fan shape. Arrange a slice of stuffed olive at one end for the eye and a fan-shaped gherkin on each side for fins. SERVES 6.

Ham and Cheese Croquettes

Illustrated on page 34

3 hard-boiled eggs
75 g/3 oz ham
25 g/1 oz margarine
25 g/1 oz plain flour
150 ml/¼ pint milk
¾ teaspoon salt
¼ teaspoon pepper
100 g/4 oz grated Cheddar cheese
1 teaspoon chopped fresh parsley
1 egg, beaten
2–3 tablespoons dried breadcrumbs
oil for deep-frying

Shell the eggs and chop them finely, together with the ham. Melt the margarine in a pan, stir in the flour and allow to cook for 1 minute. Gradually pour in the milk, stirring continuously, bring to the boil and boil the sauce for 1 minute, still stirring. Take the pan off the heat and sprinkle in the salt and pepper followed by the cheese; beat well until the cheese melts. Mix in the chopped parsley, ham and egg.

Turn the mixture on to a plate and chill it in the refrigerator for 30 minutes. With floured hands shape it into croquettes and dip each one into beaten egg before rolling it in breadcrumbs. Heat the oil for deep-frying to 180C/350F and test to see that the correct temperature has been reached by dropping a cube of bread into the pan: if it turns golden brown within 1 minute, the oil is ready. Deep-fry the croquettes for about 3 minutes until golden. Serve, if you wish, with a spicy tomato sauce. SERVES 4.

Baked Tomato Savoury

25 g/1 oz margarine
1 onion, finely chopped
225 g/8 oz tomatoes
65 g/2½ oz fresh breadcrumbs
100 g/4 oz Cheddar cheese, grated
salt and pepper · 2 teaspoons sugar

Melt the margarine in a pan and fry the onion for a few minutes, until soft. Briefly blanch the tomatoes, then peel and slice them.

Arrange the breadcrumbs, fried onion, tomato slices and cheese in alternate layers in a shallow casserole or gratin dish, sprinkling salt and pepper to taste between the layers and scattering the sugar over the tomatoes. Finish with a layer of cheese and bake the dish in a moderate oven (180 C, 350 F, gas 4) for 30–35 minutes. SERVES 4.

Stuffed Bacon Rolls

Illustrated on page 34

25 g/1 oz bacon dripping or margarine
1 small onion, finely chopped
1 small cooking apple, peeled, cored and finely chopped
50 g/2 oz fresh breadcrumbs
½ teaspoon dried sage or dried mixed herbs
8 long back bacon rashers

Melt the fat in a pan and fry the chopped onion and apple until soft but not browned. Stir in the breadcrumbs and herbs.

Derind the bacon and lay the rashers on a flat surface. Spread a little stuffing on each rasher, roll it up and secure with a wooden cocktail stick. Stand the stuffed rashers close together in a small casserole, cover and bake them in a moderately hot oven (190 C, 375 F, gas 5) for 20 minutes. Uncover and cook for another 5 minutes, until the bacon is crisp. SERVES 4.

Fish

Quick to cook, light and nutritious to eat, fish is one of the most versatile and delicious of foods. It will lend itself to all kinds of meals; a simple, satisfying fish pie, for instance, is just the right supper for a hungry family; while Trout with Orange and Herb Sauce makes a lovely dish to serve to guests.

When choosing fish, appearance is very important: the eyes should be clear, full and not sunken and the gills good and red. The flesh should be white, or faintly pink, firm in texture yet springy enough to leave no indentation when pressed with the finger. And, of course, it should always have a pleasant smell.

Fresh fish is nicest of all but it isn't always easy to obtain and so these recipes are designed to work beautifully with fresh and frozen fish alike.

Grilled Mackerel

Prepare the mackerel (allow one small fish per person) by splitting and removing the insides, washing well, and cutting off the head. Score diagonally 2 or 3 times to allow the heat to penetrate.

Brush lightly with oil and cook under a medium grill, for 10 to 15 minutes, turning over half way.

Serve with Apple or Gooseberry Sauce (page 12), thinly sliced brown bread, and butter.

Herrings can be grilled in exactly the same way.

Grilled Plaice

Clean the fish if your fishmonger has not already done so, wash and dry it well. Prepare a marinade from olive oil, a dash of lemon juice, salt and pepper and a bay leaf. The quantity required will depend on the number of fillets you have, but about a tablespoon should be sufficient for each one. Leave for 30 minutes to 1 hour, then drain.

Grill under a fairly hot grill, turning to ensure thorough cooking, until golden. Serve with Maître d'Hôtel Butter: to 100 g/4 oz softened butter, blend in 1 tablespoon chopped parsley, the juice of $\frac{1}{2}$ lemon and salt and pepper to taste.

Sole with Orange

4 sole, skinned
15 g/$\frac{1}{2}$ oz seasoned flour
50 g/2 oz butter
1 small orange, peeled and evenly sliced
1 tablespoon dry sherry
2 teaspoons cider or tarragon vinegar
chopped parsley to garnish

Wash and dry the fish very thoroughly. Coat the sole in seasoned flour. Fry gently in 40 g/1$\frac{1}{2}$ oz of the butter, allowing 5 to 8 minutes on each side, according to thickness. Keep warm in a serving dish while making the sauce: combine the orange slices, sherry and vinegar and heat gently for a few minutes in a small pan. Clean out the frying pan if necessary, put in the rest of the butter and brown it very lightly. Place the orange slices down the centre of the sole, add the sauce to the butter in the pan, stir together to blend, and pour over the fish. Garnish with chopped parsley. SERVES 4.

Herrings in Oatmeal

4 herrings, cleaned and the
boned removed
$\frac{1}{4}$ teaspoon salt
50 g/2 oz medium oatmeal
50 g/2 oz butter
juice of $\frac{1}{4}$ lemon
chopped parsley for garnish

Press the herrings into the oatmeal and salt. Fry the herrings in half the butter for 3–4 minutes each side, depending on their size. Add extra butter if necessary. Keep warm while finishing the sauce: add the remaining butter to the pan, stir in the lemon juice, heat until foaming and pour over the fish. Sprinkle with chopped parsley. SERVES 4.

Apple-stuffed Whiting with Parsley Sauce

4 smoked whiting fillets (about 675 g/1½ lb)
100 g/4 oz mushrooms
1 medium onion
1 large cooking apple
3 tablespoons chopped fresh parsley
salt and black pepper
25–50 g/1–2 oz fresh breadcrumbs (optional)
150 ml/¼ pint dry white wine or milk
Sauce
25 g/1 oz butter
25 g/1 oz flour
300 ml/½ pint milk

Cut each fillet in half lengthways. Clean and trim the mushrooms and chop them finely, together with the onion. Grate the apple. Mix together the mushrooms, onion, apple, 1 tablespoon chopped parsley and salt and pepper to taste to a smooth consistency, soft enough to spread; if it becomes too soft, add some breadcrumbs.

Spread a little stuffing on the flesh side of each half fillet and roll it up, from the head towards the tail. Secure the rolls with wooden cocktail sticks or cotton thread and place them in a casserole. Pour in the wine or milk, cover and bake the fish in a moderate oven (180 C, 350 F, gas 4) for 15–20 minutes. Lift the fish rolls out of the casserole with a straining spoon, remove the cocktail sticks or thread and keep them warm while you make the sauce.

Melt the butter in a pan, stir in the flour and cook for 1 minute. Make the liquid left in the casserole up to 450 ml/¾ pint by adding the milk and gradually pour the mixture into the pan, stirring continuously. Bring the sauce to the boil and allow it to boil for 2 minutes, still stirring, then take the pan off the heat and mix in the remaining parsley with salt and pepper to taste. Serve the sauce in a sauce boat alongside the fish. SERVES 4.

Cod Steaks with Vegetables

1 clove garlic
salt and white pepper
15 g/½ oz butter
15 g/½ oz plain flour
4 tablespoons dry white wine
4 tablespoons water
4 (225-g/8-oz) cod steaks
1 small onion · 50 g/2 oz mushrooms
1 small green pepper · 2 tomatoes
1 tablespoon olive oil
25 g/1 oz fresh breadcrumbs
chopped fresh parsley to garnish

Peel and chop the garlic clove and crush it to a paste with ¼ teaspoon salt, using the round-ended blade of a knife. Melt the butter in a pan, stir in the garlic and flour and cook them for 1 minute. Do not allow them to brown. Pour in the wine and water, bring the mixture to the boil, stirring continuously, and boil it for 2 minutes. Sprinkle in ¼ teaspoon white pepper and pour the sauce into a shallow ovenproof dish large enough to hold the cod steaks. Wipe the steaks and place them in the dish.

Slice the onion. Clean, trim and slice the mushrooms. Cut the pepper into quarters discarding the stalk, seeds and pith and slice the quarters into thin strips. Cut crosses in the bases of the tomatoes, scald them with hot water, plunge them into cold water and peel away the skins. Chop the tomatoes roughly.

Heat the oil in a small pan and fry the onion until soft but not browned. Add the sliced mushrooms and pepper and cook for 2–3 minutes. Stir in the breadcrumbs, tomatoes and a little salt and pepper and spread some of the mixture on top of each cod steak. Cover the fish with a piece of greased greaseproof paper and bake it in a moderately hot oven (200 C, 400 F, gas 6) for 25–30 minutes. Remove the paper and serve the fish sprinkled with chopped parsley. SERVES 4.

Savoury Baked Haddock

675 g / 1½ lb haddock fillets
1 tablespoon lemon juice
salt and pepper
1 medium onion
6 tomatoes
3 tablespoons finely grated Cheddar cheese
6 tablespoons fresh breadcrumbs

Arrange the haddock in a shallow ovenproof dish, having first cut any larger fillets in half. Sprinkle the fish with the lemon juice followed by a little salt and pepper.

Finely chop the onion. Cut crosses in the bases of the tomatoes, dip them briefly into hot water, plunge them into cold water and peel away the skins. Finely slice the tomatoes.

Scatter the chopped onion over the fish and lay the sliced tomatoes on top. Mix together the cheese and breadcrumbs and sprinkle the mixture liberally over the tomatoes. Bake the haddock in a moderate oven (180 C, 350 F, gas 4) for about 30 minutes, until golden. SERVES 6.

Trout with Orange and Herb Sauce

Illustrated on page 34

4 cleaned rainbow trout
40 g/1½ oz butter
salt and pepper
2 teaspoons chopped fresh parsley
2 teaspoons fresh or 1 teaspoon dried thyme
1 tablespoon chopped fresh chives
grated rind and juice of 1 large orange
4 tablespoons water
orange slices and cress for garnish

Wash the trout inside and out under cold water and wipe them dry. Remove the rack from the grill, heat the pan and grease it with 15 g/½ oz of the butter. Cut the remaining butter into flakes. Place the trout in the grill pan and dot the fish with half the butter. Grill them under a medium heat for 5 minutes, then turn them over, dot them with the remaining butter, sprinkle them with salt and pepper and cook them for a further 5 minutes.

Mix together the herbs, the orange rind and juice and the water and pour the mixture into the pan with the fish. Continue cooking under the grill for a further minute or until the sauce is heated through. Arrange the trout on a warmed serving dish, spoon over the sauce and serve hot, garnished, if you wish, with orange slices and cress. SERVES 4.

Quick Fish and Mushroom Dish

50 g/2 oz mushrooms
25 g/1 oz butter
3–4 tablespoons White Sauce (page 10)
4 (175-g/6-oz) white fish fillets (cod, haddock, whiting)
1 tablespoon chopped fresh parsley
salt and pepper
4–6 tablespoons fresh breadcrumbs

Clean, trim and chop the mushrooms. Use a quarter of the butter to grease a small, shallow ovenproof dish. Melt the rest and keep it on one side. Spread the white sauce in the bottom of the dish and arrange the fish fillets on top, followed by the chopped mushrooms. Pour over the melted butter, sprinkle the fish with the parsley and a little salt and pepper and cover the whole dish with a layer of breadcrumbs. Bake it in a moderately hot oven (190 C, 375 F, gas 5) for 15–18 minutes, until crisp and golden. SERVES 4.

Lentil Soup (page 17) and Salmon Mousse (page 22)
Overleaf Trout with Orange and Herb Sauce (page 31) and,
together on the same plate, Ham and Cheese Croquettes
(page 23) and Stuffed Bacon Rolls (page 24)

Fish Pie

575 g/1¼ lb white fish fillets (cod, coley, haddock)
50 g/2 oz margarine
1 tablespoon lemon juice
salt and pepper
450 g/1 lb peeled potatoes
about 300 ml/½ pint milk
25 g/1 oz plain flour
75 g/3 oz Cheddar cheese, grated (optional)
2 large tomatoes, sliced
15 g/½ oz butter, melted
parsley sprigs

Cut the fish fillets to fit tightly into a shallow ovenproof dish. Dot them with 15 g/½ oz of the margarine and sprinkle them with the lemon juice, ¼ teaspoon salt and a pinch of pepper. Cover the dish with cooking foil and bake the fish in a moderately hot oven (190 C, 375 F, gas 5) for about 15 minutes, until tender.

Meanwhile, cook the potatoes in plenty of boiling salted water for 20–25 minutes, until soft. Drain and mash them with another 15 g/½ oz margarine and about 2 tablespoons of the milk to give a smooth texture. Add salt to taste.

Drain any cooking liquid from the fish and make it up to 300 ml/½ pint with the rest of the milk. Melt the remaining margarine in a pan, stir in the flour and cook for 1 minute. Gradually add the milk, stirring continuously, bring the sauce to the boil and boil it for 2 minutes, still stirring. Take the pan off the heat and sprinkle in the cheese, if used, followed by salt and pepper to taste. Stir until the cheese has dissolved, then pour the sauce into the ovenproof dish, covering the fish completely. Spread the mashed potato on top with a fork, leaving a gap down the centre. Arrange the tomato slices in an overlapping row down this gap, brush the top of the pie with the melted butter and cook it under a medium grill for about 10 minutes, until the top is golden and the tomatoes are cooked. Serve it garnished with parsley. SERVES 4.

Tuna and Sweet Corn Casserole

1 (198-g/7-oz) can tuna
75 g/3 oz margarine
50 g/2 oz plain flour
300 ml/½ pint milk
¼ teaspoon salt
generous grinding of black pepper
3 heaped tablespoons fresh breadcrumbs
1 (198-g/7-oz) can sweet corn

Drain the tuna, reserving the oil, and flake the fish with a fork. Melt 40 g/1½ oz of the margarine in a pan with the oil, stir in the flour and cook for 1 minute. Gradually add the milk, stirring continuously, and bring the sauce to the boil. Allow it to boil for 2 minutes, stirring all the time and season it with the salt and pepper. Add the flaked tuna and spoon the mixture into a 900-ml/1½-pint pie dish or casserole.

Melt the remaining margarine in a clean pan and mix in the breadcrumbs. Drain the sweet corn, add it to the pan and combine everything well together. Arrange the mixture on top of the tuna and bake the casserole in a moderately hot oven (190 C, 375 F, gas 5) for 20 minutes. SERVES 4.

Favourite Meat Dishes

It's always the dishes with the simplest, most nourishing ingredients that seem to become the well-tried favourites. Roast Beef with Yorkshire Pudding, Stuffed Breast of Lamb, Steak and Kidney Pudding – all these are greeted with delight time and time again as they appear on the lunch table. A good roast joint – crisp on the outside, succulent and tender on the inside – is still a must for Sunday lunch in many people's homes and you can vary it with all sorts of different accompaniments and stuffings: sage and onion or apricot with roast pork, raisin or mint stuffing for lamb.

For lighter, weekday fare, try Kidneys with Yogurt or Lamb with Orange and Redcurrant Sauce. And of course, your Sunday joint should keep you going for a day or two – if the family doesn't demolish it at one sitting!

Roast Beef and Yorkshire Pudding

40 g/1½ oz beef dripping
1.25–1.5 kg/2½–3 lb topside of beef or rib, boned and rolled
1½ teaspoons plain flour
½ teaspoon mustard powder
Yorkshire Puddings
100 g/4 oz strong plain flour
¼ teaspoon salt
1 large egg, beaten
300 ml/½ pint milk or 200 ml/7 fl oz milk mixed with 5
tablespoons water
15 g/½ oz beef dripping
Gravy
1 tablespoon plain flour
150–300 ml/¼–½ pint stock (page 9) or vegetable water
salt and pepper

Set the oven at moderately hot (190 C, 375 F, gas 5). Put the dripping in a large roasting tin and place this in the oven until the dripping has melted and become quite hot. Add the meat to the tin and turn it over in the fat to seal it. Mix together the flour and mustard powder and sprinkle the mixture on top of the meat. Return the joint to the oven and roast it, allowing 15 minutes per 450 g/1 lb and 15 minutes over for rare beef or 20 minutes per 450 g/1 lb and 20 minutes over if you prefer your beef to be medium done.

Meanwhile prepare the batter for the Yorkshire puddings. Sift the flour and salt into a large mixing bowl and mix in the beaten egg. Gradually stir in the milk, then beat the mixture hard until it is smooth and bubbles appear. This beating is essential to enable the pudding to rise. Allow the batter to stand until it is needed but beat it well again before using it.

Remove the meat from the oven to a warm dish and turn up the oven to hot (220 C, 425 F, gas 7). Divide the dripping for the puddings between 12 deep patty tins and put these in the oven until the fat has melted and become hot. Spoon a little batter into each tin, place the tins near the top of the oven and bake the puddings for 20–30 minutes, until golden brown. Alternatively, you can cook them at the same time as the meat, above the joint. In that case, allow about 45 minutes cooking time.

Instead of making separate puddings, you can if you prefer turn the batter out into a roasting tin and bake it whole, dividing it into slices when you serve it with the joint.

While the puddings are cooking, you can make the gravy. Pour all the meat juices left in the roasting tin into a cold basin. Skim off as much fat as you can and put 2 tablespoons of it into a small pan (pour any remainder into a dripping jar). Heat the fat, stir in the flour and cook for 1 minute. Make up the meat juices to 300 ml/½ pint with stock or vegetable water, add this to the pan and bring the gravy to the boil, stirring continuously. Allow it to boil for 2 minutes, still stirring, season it to taste with salt and pepper and serve the gravy in a sauce boat alongside the roast beef and Yorkshire puddings, with horseradish sauce (page 11) if you wish. SERVES 4–6.

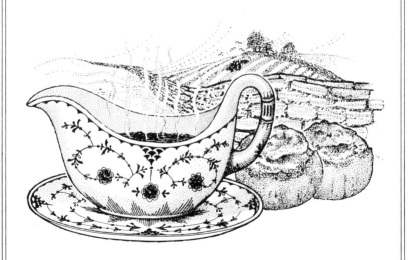

Stuffed Breast of Lamb

1 onion
225 g/8 oz sausagemeat
1 egg, beaten
1 tablespoon chopped fresh mint
75 g/3 oz fresh breadcrumbs
25 g/1 oz grated suet
$\frac{3}{4}$ teaspoon salt
$\frac{1}{4}$ teaspoon pepper
1 large breast of lamb, boned (about 675 g/1½ lb)
a little melted dripping or oil

Finely chop the onion and mix it in a bowl with the sausagemeat, beaten egg, mint, breadcrumbs, suet, salt and pepper. Remove the fat underneath the skin of the lamb and trim away any other excess fat from the meat. Spread the stuffing over the underside of the lamb, leaving a small border all round, roll up the meat and fasten it with skewers. Now tie pieces of fine string round the roll at intervals, securing the joint, and remove the skewers.

Weigh the lamb before placing it on a rack inside a roasting tin and brushing a little melted dripping or oil over the top. Roast it in a moderate oven (180 C, 350 F, gas 4), allowing 35 minutes per 450 g/1 lb of stuffed weight. Remove the string before serving. SERVES 4.

Roast Lamb with Raisin Stuffing

1 large cooking apple
1 tablespoon chutney
50 g/2 oz white breadcrumbs
1 small egg, beaten
100 g/4 oz raisins
¾ teaspoon salt
¼ teaspoon pepper
1 best end of neck of lamb, boned and chined
15 g/½ oz butter

Peel, quarter, core and finely dice the apple. Mix it in a bowl with the chutney, breadcrumbs, beaten egg, raisins and salt and pepper. Spread the stuffing evenly over the lamb and roll up the joint from the meatier side. Tie pieces of string at intervals round the joint to secure it.

Weigh the lamb, then place it in a roasting pan, dot the top with butter and roast it in a moderately hot oven (190 C, 375 F, gas 5), allowing 20–25 minutes per 450 g/1 lb and 20–25 minutes over.

Roast Pork with Sage and Onion Stuffing

A whole leg of pork makes a wonderful Sunday roast and will serve 8–10 people. If this is too much for you and you only wish to serve four, use the fillet end on its own.

1 leg of pork or 1.5 kg/3 lb fillet of leg
1 onion
1 cooking apple
75 g/3 oz fresh breadcrumbs
25 g/1 oz shredded suet
1 tablespoon chopped fresh or 2 teaspoons dried sage
salt and pepper
1 egg yolk
about 1 tablespoon oil

Ask the butcher to bone the pork for you and score the top so that it will make good crackling.

Grate the onion and apple and mix them in a bowl with the breadcrumbs, suet, sage, ¾ teaspoon salt and ¼ teaspoon pepper. Bind all the ingredients together with the egg yolk and use the mixture to stuff the cavity in the pork, securing the opening with metal or wooden skewers or sewing it up with fine string. Weigh the pork before placing it in a roasting tin. Wrap any remaining stuffing in cooking foil and put the parcel in the tin with the pork. Rub the joint all over with oil and salt to help keep the skin crisp and roast it in a moderately hot oven (190 C, 375 F, gas 5), allowing 35 minutes per 450 g/1 lb of stuffed weight.

Serve with roast potatoes, Apple Sauce (page 12) and a fresh green vegetable such as cabbage or broccoli.

Belly of Pork with Apricot Stuffing

Illustrated on page 51

There are all sorts of different stuffings you can use with pork. Here is a mild, fruit-flavoured one to serve as a change from the traditional onion stuffings.

75 g/3 oz apricots
25 g/1 oz margarine
75 g/3 oz fresh breadcrumbs
¼ teaspoon mixed spice
salt and pepper
1 tablespoon lemon juice
1 egg, beaten
1.5 kg/3 lb pork belly, boned
about 1 tablespoon oil

Soak the apricots overnight in water to cover, drain and chop them. Melt the margarine in a pan. Put the apricots, margarine, breadcrumbs, spice, ¼ teaspoon salt, ¼ teaspoon pepper, the lemon juice and egg in a bowl and mix all the ingredients well together.

Spread the stuffing on the boned side of the pork belly, roll up the meat and secure the roll at intervals with fine string. Weigh the joint, then rub the outside liberally with oil and salt and roast it in a moderately hot oven (190 C, 375 F, gas 5), allowing 35 minutes per 450 g/1 lb of stuffed weight. If towards the end of cooking time the skin is not crisping up enough, raise the oven temperature to hot (220 C, 425 F, gas 7) for the last 15 minutes before serving. SERVES 4–6.

Herb Pudding

This is an excellent accompaniment to roast pork.

1 egg
300 ml/½ pint milk
generous pinch of salt and pepper
65 g/2½ oz fresh breadcrumbs
50 g/2 oz grated suet
2 teaspoons chopped fresh parsley or ½ teaspoon each dried
sage and marjoram

Whisk together the egg, milk, salt and pepper and warm the mixture in a pan over a gentle heat, stirring until it begins to thicken. Add the breadcrumbs, suet and herbs, mix well and pour the mixture into a greased 1.15-litre/2-pint pie dish. Bake the pudding in a moderately hot oven (200 C, 400 F, gas 6) for 25–30 minutes, until golden.

Steak and Kidney Pudding

1 tablespoon plain flour
¾ teaspoon salt
¼ teaspoon pepper
450 g/1 lb lean pie beef or stewing steak
225 g/8 oz ox kidney
100 g/4 oz onion
2 tablespoons beef dripping or oil
300 ml/½ pint water
2 teaspoons Worcestershire sauce
100 g/4 oz mushrooms, sliced (optional)
Suet crust
225 g/8 oz self-raising flour
½ teaspoon salt
100 g/4 oz shredded suet
about 7 tablespoons water

Mix the flour with the salt and pepper. Cut the beef into 2.5-cm/1-in cubes and the kidney into slightly smaller chunks. Coat all the meat well with the seasoned flour. Chop the onion. Heat the dripping or oil in a pan, add the meat and onion and fry them, turning frequently, for about 2 minutes, until the pieces of meat are sealed. Stir in the water and the Worcestershire sauce and bring the mixture to the boil. Cover the pan and simmer for 1½ hours or until the meat is tender, stirring occasionally to make sure the meat is not sticking to the bottom of the pan.

To make suet crust, sift the flour and salt into a large mixing bowl and add the suet. Gradually mix in enough water to give a smooth, dough-like consistency, firm enough to roll. Lightly grease a 1.15-litre/2-pint pudding basin. Roll the dough out on a lightly floured surface to a round with a diameter of about 35 cm/14 in. Cut one quarter segment from the round and keep this on one side to make the lid. Lift the remaining piece of dough as it is into the basin; it should fit the shape of the basin exactly, with the two cut edges meeting at the side. Mould the dough into the base and round the side of the basin and pinch the edges together to seal.

When the meat is cooked, strain the gravy into a bowl or a jug and mix the sliced mushrooms, if used, into the meat. Put the mixture inside the basin lined with suet crust and add 3 tablespoons of the gravy. Roll out the remaining dough to a round to fit the top of the pudding, dampen the edges and press it on firmly, pinching the edges together to seal. Cover the surface with a piece of greased greaseproof paper, making a 2.5-cm/1-in pleat down the centre of the paper to allow the pudding to rise. Top the basin with cooking foil, pressing the foil round the rim and securing it with string. Put the basin in a steamer and stand this in a large saucepan of boiling water, making sure that the water reaches two-thirds way up the basin. Steam the pudding for 1½ hours, topping up the boiling water when necessary.

Serve the pudding straight from the basin with a napkin wrapped round it to contain the heat. Warm the reserved gravy and serve it in a sauce boat alongside. SERVES 6.

Lamb with Orange and Redcurrant Sauce

1 large onion
2 tablespoons oil
4 oranges
2 tablespoons redcurrant jelly
600 ml/1 pint chicken stock (page 9, or use a stock cube)
675 g/1½ lb cooked lamb (from the leg or shoulder)
1 teaspoon mustard powder
1 teaspoon castor sugar
generous pinch of cayenne
2 tablespoons cornflour
salt and pepper

Finely chop the onion. Heat the oil in a large saucepan and fry the onion gently until soft. Grate the rind from the oranges. Peel one orange and cut four slices from the centre, trimming away the pith. Reserve these for a garnish.

Squeeze the juice from the remaining oranges and add it to the pan with the rind, redcurrant jelly and all but 4 tablespoons of the stock. Simmer the mixture for 5 minutes.

Cut the lamb into bite-size pieces. Combine the mustard, sugar, cayenne and cornflour and whisk these ingredients into the remaining stock. Stir the mixture into the orange sauce and add the lamb followed by salt and pepper to taste. Bring the mixture to the boil, stirring, lower the heat and simmer it gently for 15 minutes.

Transfer the lamb with its sauce to a warm dish and serve it garnished with orange slices. SERVES 4–6.

Oven-fried Chicken with Corn Fritters

Illustrated on page 51

3 tablespoons seasoned flour
1 large egg, beaten · 4 chicken joints
6 tablespoons dried breadcrumbs
50 g/2 oz butter · 4 tablespoons oil
4 medium bananas · parsley sprigs to garnish
Corn fritters
150 g/5 oz plain flour · ¼ teaspoon salt
1 teaspoon cream of tartar
¼ teaspoon bicarbonate of soda
25 g/1 oz semolina
1 (198-g/7-oz) can sweet corn
1 egg · 3 tablespoons oil
4 tablespoons milk · 25 g/1 oz margarine

Brush the chicken joints all over with beaten egg, toss them in the seasoned flour and leave them to dry for about 10 minutes. Now dip them again in the egg and coat them with breadcrumbs.

Put the butter and oil in a roasting tin and heat the tin in a moderately hot oven (190 C, 375 F, gas 5) for 10 minutes. Add the chicken joints, baste them well with the fat and cook them in the oven, uncovered, for 30 minutes or until tender.

To make the corn fritters, sift the flour with the salt, cream of tartar and bicarbonate of soda and mix in the semolina. Drain the sweet corn. Beat the egg in a separate bowl and add 2 tablespoons of the oil, the milk and the sweet corn; stir this mixture into the dry ingredients and beat everything well together. Heat the remaining oil in a frying pan with the margarine and place spoonfuls of the batter in the hot fat, allowing room for the fritters to spread a little. Fry them for 2–3 minutes on each side, until golden. Cut the bananas in half lengthways, add them to the pan and fry them for a few minutes until they, too, are golden.

Arrange the chicken joints, corn fritters and fried bananas on a serving dish and garnish with parsley. SERVES 4.

Pork Penny Loaves

675 g/1½ lb minced pork or 450 g/1 lb minced pork and
225 g/½ lb bacon pieces
1 small cooking apple, grated
75 g/3 oz fresh breadcrumbs
3 tablespoons grated onion
salt, pepper and ¼ teaspoon powdered mace
1 egg, lightly beaten
about 150 ml/¼ pint stock (page 9)
1 green pepper
1 (396-g/14-oz) can tomatoes
1 tablespoon sugar
1 tablespoon vinegar
½ teaspoon mustard powder

Mix the meat in a bowl with the apple, breadcrumbs, 2 tablespoons of the onion, the seasonings and the beaten egg and stir in enough stock to bind the mixture to a smooth consistency. Using floured hands form the mixture into 8 small, loaf-shaped pieces and place these in a baking tin just large enough to hold them – about 23 × 30 cm/9 × 12 in should be right.

Quarter the green pepper, removing the stalk, seeds and pith and finely chop the quarters. Rub the tomatoes with their juice through a sieve or blend them in a liquidiser until smooth. Put the tomato purée into a pan with the chopped pepper, the remaining grated onion, the sugar, vinegar and mustard and bring the mixture to the boil. Pour the sauce over the loaves in the baking tin, place the tin in a moderately hot oven (190 C, 375 F, gas 5) and bake the loaves for 1 hour, basting them occasionally with the sauce. SERVES 4.

Kidneys with Yogurt

8 lamb's kidneys
½ green pepper
1 onion
100 g/4 oz lean bacon
100 g/4 oz mushrooms
15 g/½ oz butter
300 ml/½ pint stock (page 9) or water
1 tablespoon tomato purée
¾ teaspoon salt
¼ teaspoon pepper
1 tablespoon cornflour
1 tablespoon dry sherry
2 tablespoons natural yogurt

Remove the transparent skins from the kidneys and cut them into quarters, discarding all white gristle. Quarter the green pepper, remove the stalk, seeds and pith and cut the flesh into strips. Chop the onion. Cut the rind from the bacon and slice the rashers into thin strips. Clean, trim and quarter the mushrooms.

Melt the butter in a frying pan and fry the onion and bacon until soft. Add the kidneys and continue frying for 3 minutes. Stir in all but 2 tablespoons of the stock or water, the tomato purée and the salt and pepper. Blend the cornflour with the remaining liquid, add this to the pan and bring the mixture to the boil. Mix in the mushroom quarters, green pepper and sherry and simmer for 5–7 minutes, until the kidneys are cooked. Taste and adjust the seasoning, carefully stir in the yogurt and transfer the kidneys with their sauce to a warm serving dish. SERVES 4.

Kidneys in Red Wine

675 g/1½ lb potatoes · 100 g/4 oz margarine
1 tablespoon creamy milk (use 'top of the milk' if possible)
100 g/4 oz mushrooms
1 tablespoon plain flour
salt and pepper · 6 lamb's kidneys
150 ml/¼ pint light stock (page 9)
150 ml/¼ pint red wine
chopped fresh parsley to garnish

Peel the potatoes and cook them in plenty of boiling salted water for 20–25 minutes, until soft. Drain and mash them to a smooth purée with 40 g/1½ oz of the margarine and the milk. Spoon the potato round the inside edge of a shallow ovenproof dish or put the purée into a piping bag fitted with a large star-shaped vegetable nozzle and pipe it round the dish. Melt another 15 g/½ oz margarine and brush it over the potato. Place the dish under a low grill to keep warm.

Clean and trim the mushrooms, chopping larger ones in half. Mix the flour with ¼ teaspoon salt and a pinch of pepper. Free the kidneys from their skins and cut them into 1-cm/½-in pieces, discarding the gristly core. Toss the kidney pieces well in the seasoned flour and keep any remaining flour on one side. Melt the rest of the margarine in a frying pan, add the kidneys and stir them over a low heat until browned. Allow them to cook for 2 minutes, then put the mushrooms in the pan together with the reserved seasoned flour. Cook for a further minute before pouring in the stock and wine. Bring the mixture to the boil, stirring continuously, lower the heat and simmer it for about 10 minutes, until the kidney is tender. Taste and adjust the seasoning.

Increase the temperature of the grill to hot and continue grilling the potato until it is golden. Pour the kidneys with their sauce into the centre of the dish, sprinkle chopped fresh parsley on top and serve. SERVES 4.

Belly of Pork with Apricot Stuffing (page 43) and Oven-fried Chicken with Corn Fritters (page 47)
Overleaf Rabbit Cobbler (page 64) and Tomato and Cheese Soufflé (page 72)

Casseroles and Bakes

A good, meaty casserole makes a welcome main meal for any time of the day, whether it is a lunch to keep you going during a hard day's work or a warming, relaxing supper in front of the fire. And it makes an economical meal too, as even the cheapest, toughest cuts of meat can be cooked to a melting tenderness, producing a rich, delicious gravy, as long as you stew them slowly at a low enough temperature.

A little meat can go a long way, however, and often the tastiest supper dishes of all are savoury mixtures of potatoes, eggs, a few strips of bacon or ham or a small portion of mince and a generous sprinkling of grated cheese, all baked to a crisp, golden and appetising meal. Children especially love baked suppers.

Stuffed Beef Roll

1 onion
25–50 g/1–2 oz dripping
50 g/2 oz rolled oats or fresh breadcrumbs
1 small egg, beaten
25 g/1 oz shredded suet
salt and pepper
575–675 g/1¼–½ lb piece of braising steak, 1 cm/½ in thick
2 teaspoons Worcestershire sauce
1 tablespoon plain flour
1 (227-g/8-oz) can tomatoes
about 150 ml/¼ pint stock (page 9 or use a stock cube)

First make the stuffing. Finely chop the onion. Heat 25 g/1 oz of the dripping or oil in a pan and fry the onion until soft but not browned. Drain the onion into a bowl and combine it with the oats or breadcrumbs, the beaten egg, suet, ¾ teaspoon salt and ¼ teaspoon pepper.

Lay the steak on a board and flatten it with a meat hammer or a rolling pin. Sprinkle it with the Worcestershire sauce. Spread the stuffing over the meat to within 1 cm/½ in of the edge, roll the steak up into a neat shape and tie string round the roll at intervals to secure it. Season the flour and roll the steak in the mixture. Reserve any remaining seasoned flour.

Add some more fat to the pan, if necessary, heat it and fry the beef roll briskly in the fat for a few minutes, turning frequently, until sealed on all sides. Transfer it to a casserole just large enough to hold it. Stir any remaining seasoned flour into the fat in the pan and cook for 1 minute, stirring. Pour in the tomatoes with their juice followed by the stock (you will need to add enough stock to bring the liquid half way up the meat). Bring the mixture to the boil, pour it over the meat and adjust the stock as necessary. Cover and cook in a moderate oven (160 C, 325 F, gas 3) for about 2 hours, until tender.

Put the beef roll on a warm serving dish. Pour any remaining stock into a clean pan with the liquid from the casserole, bring to the boil and simmer for a few minutes, until the mixture is reduced to a rich gravy. Serve the gravy in a sauce boat alongside the meat. SERVES 4–6.

Spicy Beef

575–675 g/1¼–1½ lb chuck steak
25 g/1 oz plain flour
1 tablespoon curry powder
½ teaspoon salt
2–3 tablespoons dripping or oil
1 large onion
1 tablespoon Worcestershire sauce
1 teaspoon ground ginger
1 teaspoon brown sugar
600 ml/1 pint stock (page 9)
2 teaspoons lemon juice
50 g/2 oz dried apricots, chopped
50 g/2 oz sultanas

Cut the steak into 2.5-cm/1-in cubes, trimming away any fat. Mix together the flour, curry powder and salt and toss the meat in the mixture to coat it thoroughly. Reserve any remaining seasoned flour on one side.

Heat half the dripping or oil in a pan and fry the meat in it until well browned. Transfer it to a 1.75-litre/3-pint or a 2-litre/3½-pint casserole. Slice the onion. Put the remaining fat in the pan and soften the onion for 3–4 minutes, then stir in the Worcestershire sauce, ginger, sugar and any remaining seasoned flour. Cook for 1 minute, stirring. Gradually add the stock, lemon juice, apricots and sultanas and bring the mixture to the boil, stirring continuously. Pour it over the meat, cover the casserole and cook it in a moderate oven (180 C, 350 F, gas 4) for about 2½ hours, until the meat is tender. SERVES 4.

Pot Roast of Beef

I have included a marinade in this recipe as it really does ensure a delicious result, though you can cook the beef without it. This marinade is ideal for any of the larger and tougher cuts of meat or game.

Marinade
1 onion
6 peppercorns
4 parsley stalks
1 bay leaf
150 ml/¼ pint dry red wine
2 tablespoons olive oil
Pot roast
1.4–1.6 kg/3–3½ lb brisket of beef
2 small onions
2 sticks celery
2 carrots
3 tomatoes
½ clove garlic
2 teaspoons dripping or oil
1 bay leaf
5 peppercorns
2–3 parsley sprigs
1 teaspoon salt
generous grinding of pepper
½ teaspoon paprika

Begin by making the marinade. Slice the onion. Crush the peppercorns and parsley stalks slightly and mix them with the onion, bay leaf, wine and oil. Put the beef in a large, shallow dish and pour over the marinade. Cover and leave to stand for at least 3–4 hours, turning the meat in the marinade from time to time. Remove the meat from the bowl, strain the marinade through a fine sieve and keep it on one side.

Finely slice the onions for the pot roast. Trim and finely chop the celery and carrots. Cut crosses in the bases of the tomatoes, plunge them briefly into hot water, then into cold water and peel away the skins. Peel and crush the garlic.

Heat the fat in a heavy pan and brown the meat quickly on all sides. Lift it out of the pan and leave it on one side. Put all the prepared vegetables in the pan and cook them gently until the fat is absorbed. Now transfer the vegetables to a casserole if you intend cooking the dish in the oven, or leave them in the pan. Add the bay leaf, peppercorns, parsley and 6 tablespoons of the strained marinade or water. Lay the beef on top, sprinkle it with the salt, pepper and paprika and cover the pan or casserole tightly. Simmer it over a low heat for about 3 hours, until the meat is tender. Alternatively, cook the beef in a moderate oven (160 C, 325 F, gas 3) until the liquid just begins to bubble, then lower the heat to cool (140 C, 275 F, gas 1). The lid can be removed and the oven temperature turned up to moderately hot (200 C, 400 F, gas 6) 10 minutes before serving to allow the meat to crisp up.

Strain the vegetables and cooking liquid to serve as gravy. If you like, you can thicken the gravy with a little plain flour in a pan: bring the mixture to the boil and boil it for 2 minutes, stirring, before pouring it into a sauce boat and serving it with the meat. SERVES 6.

Lamb Casserole with Parsley Dumplings

2 carrots
1 onion
2 sticks celery
2 tablespoons oil or dripping
4 large lamb chops
1 tablespoon plain flour
1 (396-g/14-oz) can tomatoes
1 teaspoon dried mixed herbs
salt and black pepper
Dumplings
100 g/4 oz self-raising flour
$\frac{1}{4}$ teaspoon salt
50 g/2 oz shredded suet
1 tablespoon chopped fresh parsley

Peel and chop the carrots and onion. Cut the celery into 2.5-cm/1-in lengths. Heat the oil or dripping in a pan and gently fry the onion, carrot and celery for 5 minutes. Transfer the vegetables to a 1.4-litre/2$\frac{1}{2}$-pint casserole.

Coat the lamb chops in the flour, brown them quickly in the pan and arrange them over the vegetables. Sprinkle any remaining flour into the pan and cook gently for 1 minute, stirring continuously. Add the tomatoes with their juice followed by 150 ml/$\frac{1}{4}$ pint water, herbs and salt and pepper to taste. Bring the mixture to the boil and pour it into the casserole. Cover and cook the casserole in a moderate oven (180 C, 350 F, gas 4) for 1 hour.

Meanwhile, prepare the dumplings. Mix all the ingredients together in a bowl, adding just enough cold water to form a soft but not sticky dough. With floured hands shape this into eight dumplings. Increase the oven temperature to moderately hot (200 C, 400 F, gas 6), remove the cover from the lamb and drop the dumplings into the boiling liquid. (If your casserole is flameproof, the whole of the dish can be cooked on the hob.) Allow the dumplings to cook for 20 minutes and serve. SERVES 4.

Lamb Casserole with Cheesy Topping

675 g/1½ lb stewing lamb
2 onions
4 sticks celery
3–4 carrots
450 ml/¾ pint stock (page 9, or use a stock cube)
salt and pepper
Topping
225 g/8 oz self-raising flour
pinch of salt
1 teaspoon mustard powder
50 g/2 oz margarine
175 g/6 oz Cheddar cheese, grated
150 ml/¼ pint milk

Cut the lamb into bite-sized pieces, trimming away excess fat. Slice the onions. Trim and chop the celery and carrots. Arrange the lamb and vegetables in layers in a casserole, pour in the stock and sprinkle in salt and pepper to taste. Cover the casserole and cook it in a moderate oven (180 C, 350 F, gas 4) for 1¼ hours.

Sift the flour, salt and mustard into a large mixing bowl. Rub in the margarine, stir in all but 50 g/2 oz of the cheese and mix all the ingredients to a soft dough with the milk, reserving 1 tablespoon of milk for a glaze. On a lightly floured surface, roll the dough out to a round to fit the top of the casserole and cut the round into eight triangular segments. Take the casserole out of the oven, remove the lid and arrange the pastry segments on top of the meat. Brush them with the remaining milk and sprinkle them with the rest of the cheese. Raise the oven temperature to moderately hot (200 C, 400 F, gas 6), return the casserole to the oven and cook it for a further 20–25 minutes, until the topping is nicely browned. SERVES 4.

Pork in Cider

675 g/1½ lb lean pork
25 g/1 oz plain flour
1 medium onion
1 large dessert apple
25 g/1 oz margarine
finely grated rind and juice of ½ lemon
1 bay leaf
300 ml/½ pint dry cider
salt and pepper

Cut the pork into cubes and toss them in the flour, coating them generously. Slice the onion. Peel, core and slice the apple. Melt the margarine in a frying pan and fry the pork until browned on all sides. Lift the meat out with a slotted spoon and transfer it to a casserole.

Fry the onion gently until it begins to colour, then add it to the pork with the sliced apple, the lemon rind and juice, bay leaf and cider. Sprinkle in salt and pepper to taste, cover the casserole and cook it in a moderately hot oven (190 C, 375 F, gas 5) for about 1½ hours, until the meat is tender. SERVES 4.

Sherried Chicken Casserole

50 g/2 oz butter
4 large chicken joints
2 rashers back bacon
1 medium onion
100–175 g/4–6 oz mushrooms
40 g/1½ oz plain flour
300 ml/½ pint chicken stock (page 9, or use a stock cube)
1½ tablespoons tomato purée
2 tablespoons dry sherry
salt and pepper
225 g/8 oz brown rice
chopped fresh parsley to garnish

Melt the butter in a large frying pan, add the chicken joints and fry them gently for about 10 minutes, turning once, until they are golden brown. Transfer them to a saucepan or a flameproof casserole, preferably a large, shallow one which holds all the joints in one layer.

Remove the rind from the bacon and chop the rashers, together with the onion. Add these to the pan and fry them until they are just beginning to colour. Clean and trim the mushrooms, cut larger ones in half and put them in the pan. Continue cooking for 2 minutes. Sprinkle in the flour and allow it to cook for 1 minute, stirring continuously.

Heat the stock, mix in the tomato purée and pour the liquid into the pan. Bring to the boil, stirring, and add the sherry followed by salt and pepper to taste. Pour the mixture over the chicken, cover the casserole and simmer it gently for 45 minutes – 1 hour, until the chicken is cooked.

Meanwhile, wash the rice and cook it in plenty of boiling salted water for 20–30 minutes, until it is cooked but still has a 'bite' to it. Drain the rice, arrange it around the edge of a large serving dish and pile the chicken joints in the centre. Pour the sauce over the top, sprinkle with chopped fresh parsley and serve. SERVES 4.

Chicken and Rice Casserole

2 sticks celery
1 onion
65 g/2½ oz butter
4 chicken joints
225 g/8 oz long grain rice
1 (396-g/14 oz) can tomatoes
600 ml/1 pint stock (page 9, or use a stock cube)
1 teaspoon dried mixed herbs
1 teaspoon sugar
100 g/4 oz mushrooms
salt and pepper

Trim the celery sticks and chop them finely, together with the onion. Melt all but 15 g/½ oz of the butter in a large pan and brown the chicken joints on all sides. Lift them out with a slotted spoon and transfer them to a casserole. Put the celery, onion and rice in the pan and sauté gently for about 3 minutes, stirring from time to time. Pour in the tomatoes with their juice, the stock, herbs and sugar and bring the mixture to the boil, stirring continuously. Season it with salt and pepper to taste and pour it into the casserole with the chicken. Cover and cook in a moderately hot oven (190 C, 375 F, gas 5) for 1 hour.

Just before the end of cooking time, slice the mushrooms and sauté them in the remaining butter for 1–2 minutes. Stir them into the casserole, taste and adjust the seasoning and serve. SERVES 4.

Turkey and Apple Bake

225 g/8 oz cooked turkey meat
100 g/4 oz ham
450 g/1 lb potatoes
2 large cooking apples
2 onions
salt and pepper
300 ml/½ pint good turkey stock (page 9)
sprinkling of grated nutmeg
25 g/1 oz fresh breadcrumbs
25 g/1 oz butter

Chop or coarsely mince the turkey and ham. Parboil the potatoes in boiling salted water for 10 minutes, drain and slice them. Peel, core and finely slice the apples together with the onions. Arrange all the prepared ingredients in layers in a greased casserole, sprinkling them with salt and pepper to taste and finishing with a layer of potato.

Heat the stock, whisk in the nutmeg and pour the liquid into the casserole. Sprinkle the top with breadcrumbs, dot with butter and bake the casserole in a moderate oven (180 C, 350 F, gas 4) for about 40 minutes, until all the ingredients are tender. SERVES 4.

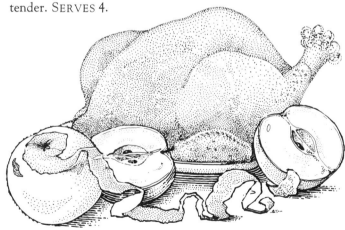

Rabbit Cobbler

Illustrated on page 52

2 tablespoons dripping or oil
4 rabbit joints
1 onion
1 carrot
1 tablespoon plain flour
450 ml/$\frac{3}{4}$ pint chicken stock (page 9, or use a stock cube)
salt and pepper
50 g/2 oz shelled fresh or frozen peas
or 1 (113-g/4-oz) packet frozen peas and carrots
Topping
175 g/6 oz self-raising flour
$\frac{1}{2}$ teaspoon salt
40 g/1$\frac{1}{2}$ oz margarine
about 150 ml/$\frac{1}{4}$ pint milk

Heat the fat in a large frying pan and fry the rabbit joints until browned on all sides. Lift them out with a slotted spoon and transfer them to a 1.4-litre/2$\frac{1}{2}$-pint casserole.

Chop the onion. Trim and slice the carrot, if used. Fry the onion in the pan until soft, add the flour and mix well. Gradually stir in the stock and bring the mixture to the boil, stirring continuously. Add the sliced carrot followed by salt and pepper to taste and pour the mixture over the rabbit. Cover the casserole and cook it in a moderate oven (180 C, 350 F, gas 4) for 1 hour or until the rabbit is just tender.

To make the topping, sift the flour and salt together into a bowl and rub in the margarine. Add enough milk to mix all the ingredients to a soft dough and roll the dough out on a floured board to a shape to fit the top of the casserole. Cut the shape into eight triangular segments.

Take the casserole out of the oven and turn up the oven temperature to hot (220 C, 425 F, gas 7). Stir in the peas or the mixed peas and carrots and lay the pastry segments on top. Brush them with a little milk. Return the casserole to the oven and cook it uncovered for a further 20 minutes, until the topping is golden brown. SERVES 4.

Farmhouse Cobbler

450 g/1 lb sausagemeat
25 g/1 oz lard or bacon dripping
2 medium onions · 2 carrots
1 potato · 1 tablespoon plain flour
1 teaspoon meat extract · pinch of salt
generous grinding of pepper
Topping
225 g/8 oz self-raising flour
pinch of salt · 50 g/2 oz margarine
75 g/3 oz Cheddar cheese, finely grated
just over 150 ml/¼ pint milk

With floured hands form the sausagemeat into 16–20 small balls. Melt the lard or dripping in a pan and fry the sausagemeat balls gently for a few minutes, turning frequently, until they are golden brown. Drain them and transfer them to a casserole.

Slice the onions into thin rings. Trim and finely slice the carrots. Peel the potato and cut it into large pieces. Put all the vegetables into the pan and fry them for 5 minutes. Stir in the flour. Dissolve the meat extract in 450 ml/¾ pint boiling water, gradually add the liquid to the pan and bring the mixture to the boil, stirring continuously. Sprinkle in the seasoning. Pour the mixture into the casserole with the sausagemeat, cover and cook in a moderately hot oven (190 C, 375 F, gas 5) for 40 minutes.

To make the topping, sift together the flour and salt and rub in the margarine. Add half the cheese followed by enough milk to bind all the ingredients to a soft but not sticky dough. Keep the remaining milk on one side for a glaze. Roll the dough out on a lightly floured surface and cut out 5-cm/2-in rounds, using a plain or fluted pastry cutter.

Take the casserole out of the oven and turn the oven temperature up to hot (220 C, 425 F, gas 7). Arrange the pastry pieces round the inside edge of the casserole, brush them with milk and sprinkle them with the remaining cheese. Bake the cobbler in the hot oven for about 10 minutes, until the topping is golden brown. SERVES 4–6.

Liver and Bacon Casserole

450–675 g/1–1½ lb potatoes
1 large onion
25 g/1 oz pork or bacon dripping or margarine
450 g/1 lb lamb's liver
3–4 rashers streaky bacon
100 g/4 oz mushrooms
2 teaspoons chopped fresh or 1 teaspoon dried sage
salt and pepper
250 ml/8 fl oz hot stock (page 9, or use a stock cube)
15 g/½ oz butter, melted

Peel the potatoes and cut them into 1-cm/½-in thick slices. Cook them in boiling salted water for 5 minutes, drain and leave them on one side.

Slice the onion into fine rings. Melt the dripping or margarine in a frying pan and fry the onion until soft. Wipe the liver, cut it into thin slices and add the slices to the hot pan, pushing the onion to one side. Fry the liver quickly until sealed, then transfer it to a casserole.

Remove the rind from the bacon. Clean and trim the mushrooms, chopping larger ones in half. Lay the onion rings, bacon rashers and mushrooms on top of the liver and sprinkle them with the sage and salt and pepper to taste. Pour over the stock. Arrange the potato slices in an overlapping layer on top, brush them with the melted butter and sprinkle them lightly with salt. Cook the casserole in a moderately hot oven (190C, 375F, gas 5) for about 1 hour, until the liver is tender. SERVES 4–6.

Apple Toad-in-the-hole

100 g/4 oz plain flour
½ teaspoon salt
1 teaspoon dried sage
1 large egg, beaten
300 ml/½ pint milk
450 g/1 lb pork sausages
2 medium cooking apples
pinch of pepper

Mix the flour, half the salt and the sage together in a mixing bowl and stir in the egg. Add half the milk and beat all the ingredients well together until the batter is thick and smooth. Now gradually beat in the remaining milk and leave the batter on one side.

Grease a small roasting tin and arrange the sausages in it. Peel the apples, cut each into eight wedges and remove the cores. Put the apple wedges in the roasting tin and sprinkle the rest of the salt and the pepper on top. Place the tin in a hot oven (220 C, 425 F, gas 7) for 10 minutes. Beat the batter briefly one more time, pour it over the sausages and apple and bake the toad-in-the-hole for a further 40 minutes or until well-risen and golden brown. SERVES 4.

Sausage and Tomato Pie

675 g/1½ lb potatoes
40 g/1½ oz margarine
salt
a little grated nutmeg
1 large onion
1 tablespoon bacon or pork dripping or oil
450 g/1 lb sausages
1 (227-g/8 oz) can tomatoes
1 tablespoon chopped fresh parsley
50 g/2 oz Cheddar cheese, grated

Peel the potatoes and boil them in plenty of salted water for 20–25 minutes, until tender. Drain and mash them with 25 g/1 oz of the margarine and salt and nutmeg to taste. Grease a medium-sized, shallow ovenproof dish and line the base and sides with two-thirds of the mashed potato.

Chop the onion. Heat the dripping or oil in a pan and fry the sausages for 10 minutes, turning them from time to time. Remove them to a plate, put the onion in the pan and fry it gently until soft. Cut all but three of the sausages into pieces and arrange these on the potato. Pour over the tomatoes, sprinkle with the parsley and onion and spread the rest of the potato on top. Slice the remaining sausages in half lengthways and place them on the potato. Melt the rest of the margarine and brush it over the pie, then sprinkle the grated cheese in between the sausages. Bake the pie in a moderate oven (180 C, 350 F, gas 4) for about 15 minutes. SERVES 4–6.

Cottage Pie

450 g/1 lb cold cooked beef or raw minced beef
1 onion
1 tablespoon dripping or oil
150–300 ml/¼–½ pint water or stock
(page 9, or use a stock cube)
salt and pepper
675 g/1½ lb potatoes
4–6 tablespoons milk
40 g/1½ oz margarine, softened

Finely chop or mince the cooked beef, if used. Chop the onion. Heat the dripping or oil in a pan and fry the onion until golden. Now stir in the cooked beef and fry it gently with the onion for a few minutes. If you are using raw minced beef, add it to the pan and fry it until well-browned, then cover the pan and simmer the meat very gently for 25–30 minutes, until tender.

Pour the water or stock into the pan, the exact amount depending on how soft you like the mixture, season with salt and pepper to taste and continue cooking for a few minutes.

Peel the potatoes and cook them in plenty of boiling salted water for 20–25 minutes, until tender. Drain and mash them with the milk and 25 g/1 oz of the margarine, adding salt and pepper to taste. Transfer the meat to a pie or soufflé dish and cover it with the mashed potato, forking the potato neatly into place. Melt the remaining margarine, brush it on top of the pie and bake the pie in a moderately hot oven (190 C, 375 F, gas 5) for about 20 minutes, until crisp and golden brown on top. SERVES 4–6.

Ham and Leeks in Cheese Sauce

4 leeks
65 g/2½ oz margarine
50 g/2 oz plain flour
300 ml/½ pint milk
sprinkling of grated nutmeg
salt and pepper
100 g/4 oz Cheddar cheese, grated
4 slices ham
2 tablespoons dried breadcrumbs
parsley sprigs to garnish (optional)

Trim and thoroughly wash the leeks and cook them in boiling salted water to cover for 15–20 minutes, until just tender. Drain, reserving the cooking liquid.

Melt all but 15 g/½ oz of the margarine in a pan, stir in the flour and cook for 1 minute. Measure 150 ml/¼ pint of the cooking liquid from the leeks and gradually pour this into the pan followed by the milk, stirring continuously. Bring the sauce to the boil, stirring, and boil it for 2 minutes, until it thickens. Take the pan off the heat, sprinkle in the nutmeg followed by salt and pepper to taste and add half the cheese. Mix well until the cheese has dissolved.

Wrap a slice of ham around each leek and arrange the leeks close together in a lightly greased, shallow ovenproof dish. Pour over the sauce. Mix the rest of the cheese with the breadcrumbs, sprinkle the mixture on top of the sauce and dot with the remaining margarine. Place the leeks under a medium grill or bake them in a moderately hot oven (190 C, 375 F, gas 5) for 20–25 minutes, until golden grown on top. Serve garnished with parsley sprigs, if liked. SERVES 4.

Wonder Bake

½ bloomer loaf, cut lengthways
1 egg, beaten
1 small onion
1 tablespoon dripping or oil
225 g/8 oz minced beef
¼ teaspoon salt
generous pinch of pepper
1 teaspoon mustard
50 g/2 oz Cheddar cheese, grated
1 (100-g/3.53-oz) packet processed cheese slices

Scoop 50 g/2 oz soft breadcrumbs out of the loaf and soak them in the beaten egg for a few minutes.

Chop the onion. Heat the dripping or oil in a pan and fry the onion until soft, then add the meat and continue cooking for a few minutes until the meat is browned all over. Stir in the salt, pepper, mustard, grated cheese and the breadcrumb and egg mixture.

Place a double sheet of cooking foil large enough to enclose the loaf on a baking tray and stand the loaf crust-side down on it. Pack the filling into the loaf and bring up the foil all round to cover it. Seal well and bake it in a moderate oven (180 C, 350 F, gas 4) for 45 minutes. Unfold the cooking foil, arrange slices of processed cheese along the top of the loaf and return it to the oven for about 5 minutes or until the cheese begins to melt. Serve with grilled tomatoes and a green vegetable. SERVES 4.

Tomato and Cheese Soufflé

Illustrated on page 52

50 g/2 oz fresh breadcrumbs
1 (142-ml/5-fl oz) carton single cream
15 g/½ oz butter
3 large tomatoes
¾ teaspoon salt
¼ teaspoon pepper
¼ teaspoon mustard powder
pinch of cayenne
100 g/4 oz Cheddar cheese, grated
2 large eggs, separated

Set the oven at moderately hot (190 C, 375 F, gas 5). Soak the breadcrumbs in the cream for 5–6 minutes.

Use the butter to grease a 15-cm/6-in soufflé dish. Cut crosses in the bases of the tomatoes, plunge them first into hot water for a few minutes, then into cold and peel away the skins. Slice the tomatoes, lay them in the base of the soufflé dish and sprinkle salt and pepper on top.

Stir the mustard and cayenne into the breadcrumb mixture and beat in the cheese followed by the egg yolks. Whisk the egg whites until stiff but not dry. Fold them carefully into the cheese mixture and pour this on top of the tomatoes in the dish. Put the dish at once into the oven and bake it for 40–45 minutes, until well risen and golden brown. Serve immediately. SERVES 4.

Salads, Vegetables and Accompaniments

A salad doesn't have to be an accompaniment: it can be a main meal in itself and often this is just the kind of meal you want. On a hot summer's day you can prepare a healthy, refreshing lunch or supper without much effort or cooking time; while in winter, when fresh vegetables are hard to come by you can keep the family fit and cheerful with colourful combinations of raw white cabbage with red apple or celery with orange, served as a side dish or a main meal, depending on what other ingredients you include.

No one would think of vegetables as unusual accompaniments with meat dishes unless they are served in unusual ways. I couldn't resist including two very out-of-the-ordinary recipes for simple garden produce: Marrow Curd and Beetroot in Jelly. They may sound strange but do try them – you will find them quite delicious!

Prawn and Ham Salad

100 g/4 oz frozen or canned prawns
175 g/6 oz brown or white long-grain rice
2 tablespoons oil
1 tablespoon wine vinegar or cider vinegar
pinch each of salt, pepper and sugar
100 g/4 oz ham, unsliced
100 g/4 oz cooked peas

Allow the frozen prawns to thaw at toom temperature, following the instructions on the packet. Otherwise, drain the canned prawns and rinse them through with cold water.

Wash the brown rice, if used, under cold running water. Cook the brown or white rice in plenty of fast boiling salted water for 22–25 minutes if brown, or 12–14 minutes if white, until tender. Drain and rinse through with cold water.

Whisk together the oil, vinegar and seasonings. Tip the rice into a salad bowl and stir in the dressing. Dice the ham and mix it into the rice with the prawns and peas. Allow the salad to stand in the refrigerator for about 1 hour before serving. SERVES 4.

Rice Salad with Stuffed Eggs

Illustrated on page 85

4 hard-boiled eggs
25 g/1 oz butter, softened
50 g/2 oz Cheddar cheese, finely grated
salt and pepper
1 teaspoon chopped fresh parsley *or*
a sprinkling of paprika
175 g/6 oz long-grain rice
1 (113-g/4-oz) packet frozen mixed vegetables
2–3 tablespoons mayonnaise or salad cream
3 tomatoes
sprigs of watercress to garnish

Shell the eggs, cut them in half lengthways and take out the yolks. Mash these until smooth with the butter, cheese and salt and pepper to taste. Transfer the mixture to a piping bag fitted with a large star-shaped nozzle and pipe the yolk back into the whites or simply pack a little into each white with a teaspoon, scoring the top of the yolk with a fork. Put the stuffed eggs on a plate and sprinkle them with parsley or a little paprika.

Cook the rice in boiling salted water for 12–14 minutes, until tender, drain and rinse through with cold water. Cook the vegetables following the instructions on the packet, drain and mix them into the rice with the mayonnaise or salad cream. Pile the rice salad on to a serving dish and place the stuffed eggs on top. Slice the tomatoes and arrange the slices around the edge of the dish, garnishing them with sprigs of watercress. SERVES 4.

Ham, Pineapple and Sweet Corn Salad

175 g/6 oz brown or white long-grain rice
1 large onion · 3 tablespoons oil
225 g/8 oz ham, unsliced
1 (198-g/7 oz) can sweet corn
2–3 fresh or canned pineapple rings
1 tablespoon chopped fresh parsley
1 tablespoon white wine vinegar or cider vinegar
½ teaspoon mustard
2 tablespoons pineapple juice
salt and pepper
a few lettuce leaves (optional)

Cook the brown or white rice until tender (see Prawn and Ham Salad, page 74), drain and leave to cool.

Chop the onion. Heat 1 tablespoon of the oil in a pan and fry the onion until soft but not browned, drain and mix it in a bowl with the rice. Dice the ham. Drain the sweet corn. Cut each pineapple ring into about eight pieces and add these to the rice with the ham, sweet corn and parsley. Mix all the ingredients well together.

Beat the vinegar with the remaining oil, the mustard, pineapple juice and salt and pepper to taste. Stir the dressing into the salad. Stand the salad in a cool place until needed and serve it on a bed of lettuce leaves, if liked. SERVES 4.

Chicken and Sweet Corn Salad

175 g/6 oz long-grain rice
225–275 g/8–10 oz cooked chicken
1 (198-g/7-oz) can sweet corn
1 small green pepper
3 tablespoons olive oil
1 tablespoon lemon juice
salt and pepper to taste

Cook the rice in plenty of boiling salted water for about 12 minutes until it is just tender but still has a bite to it. Drain, rinse it through with cold water and leave it to cool.

Cut the chicken into small pieces, reserving a few pieces of breast cut 5 cm/2 in long and 1 cm/½ in wide for garnish. Drain the sweet corn. Slice the stalk off the pepper, remove the seeds and pith and cut the pepper into fine strips. Mix the rice, chicken, sweet corn and pepper together in a bowl. Make a dressing with the oil, lemon juice and salt and pepper to taste, pour it over the salad and garnish with the reserved pieces of chicken. SERVES 4.

Variation

Chicken and Grape Salad. Omit the sweet corn and green pepper and use 175 g/6 oz green grapes, 4 tomatoes, 6 stuffed olives and 1 spring onion instead. Halve and deseed the grapes, slice the tomatoes, olives and spring onion and mix all these ingredients in the bowl with the rice and chicken. Pour over the dressing and serve.

Winter Salad

350 g/12 oz white cabbage
3 sticks celery
1 red dessert apple
50 g/2 oz raisins
50 g/2 oz walnuts, chopped
3–4 tablespoons mayonnaise

Finely shred the cabbage. Trim and slice the celery. Quarter, core and finely chop the apple. Mix all the chopped ingredients in a bowl with the raisins and walnuts and stir in the mayonnaise. Allow the salad to stand for a short while, if possible, before serving. SERVES 4–6.

Ham and Cabbage Salad

450 g/1 lb white cabbage
2 large oranges
225 g/8 oz tomatoes
225 g/8 oz ham, unsliced
4 tablespoons oil
2 tablespoons white or wine vinegar
pinch each of salt, pepper, sugar and mustard powder
chopped fresh parsley to garnish

Finely shred the cabbage. Peel the oranges, removing as much of the pith as you can, and slice the fruit. Cut the tomatoes into wedges. Dice the ham. Mix all the prepared ingredients together in a bowl.
    Whisk the oil with the vinegar, salt, pepper, sugar and mustard and pour the dressing over the salad. Sprinkle with chopped fresh parsley before serving. SERVES 8.

Baked Potatoes

Wash and dry some large, old potatoes. Prick the skins with a fork, and rub a little butter all over. Bake in a moderately hot oven 190 C, 375 F, gas 5, for 1–1½ hours depending on their size. When the potatoes are ready they should feel soft if gently squeezed. Wrapped in cloth, they will keep hot for a little while. To serve them, cut a deep cross on the top, squeeze the potato to open it out, sprinkle with salt and pepper and place a knob of butter inside.

Two Toppings for Baked Potatoes

1. Serve with soured (or fresh) cream, mixed with chopped spring onion or chives. Dust with cayenne pepper to finish.

2. Make a savoury scrambled egg topping. For each potato, warm a knob of butter and a tablespoon of cream in a small pan. Add a beaten egg, plenty of salt and pepper and lightly scramble. Stir in a little crisply fried bacon, a few peeled prawns, or chopped fresh herbs.

Roast Potatoes

Cut some peeled, old potatoes into halves or quarters, depending on their size. Dry well, put into the roasting tin with the joint of meat, baste from time to time with the fat in the tin, and turn them over to brown all sides. Allow about 1½ hours roasting time.

Alternatively, the potatoes can be boiled first for 5 to 6 minutes, drained, and placed in a roasting tin containing very hot fat. They can then be cooked on the top shelf of the oven, and will take about 1 hour to cook. Again, turn over to brown all sides.

Potato Croquettes

450 g/1 lb potatoes, weighed after peeling
25 g/1 oz butter · 1 egg, separated
¼ teaspoon nutmeg · salt and pepper
2 teaspoons finely chopped parsley
flour · dried breadcrumbs for coating

Boil, drain and mash the potatoes, beating well to eliminate
any lumps. Add the butter, egg yolk, nutmeg, salt and pepper
and parsley. Beat well to combine: the mixture should be firm
enough to handle and hold its shape well.

Form the potato purée into cork-shaped pieces, 7.5 cm/3 in
long and 2.5 cm/1 inch in diameter. Roll in flour, dip in lightly
beaten egg white, and roll in dried breadcrumbs.

Deep-fry for 3 to 4 minutes until golden, then drain on
kitchen paper. SERVES 4.

Scalloped Potatoes

4 or 5 medium sized potatoes
40 g/1½ oz butter
25 g/1 oz flour
salt and pepper
pinch of nutmeg
about 150 ml/¼ pint milk

Peel and thinly slice the potatoes, place them in a bowl of cold
water and leave for about 10 minutes. Drain and dry well.
Lightly butter a shallow, ovenproof dish. Mix together the
flour, salt, pepper and nutmeg. Arrange a layer of potato in
the bottom and sprinkle with the flour mixture. Continue in
this way, ending with potatoes on top. Dot with the
remainder of the butter.

Set the oven at 190 C, 375 F, gas 5. Pour over enough milk to
come just below the surface of the potatoes, cover (foil will
do) and cook in the heated oven for about 1 hour. Uncover
and cook for a further 30 minutes until the top is golden and
the potatoes are tender. SERVES 4.

Baked Parsnips

Parsnips are traditionally served with roast beef, together with roast potatoes.

Wash and peel the required amount of parsnips (you will need 675 g/1½ lb for 4 servings). Remove the hard core from the centre, and cut lengthwise into quarters. Sprinkle on a little salt and pepper mixed into some plain flour, and place them in a roasting tin with the meat (they are particularly good with roast beef and lamb), basting from time to time with the fat in the tin. This could take an hour depending on the heat of the oven. Parsnips are better well cooked than undercooked.

Vegetable Omelette

25 g/1 oz margarine
1 teaspoon oil
1 small onion, thinly sliced
1 small potato, cooked and finely chopped
1 tomato, skinned and coarsely chopped
50 g/2 oz mushrooms, chopped
½ green pepper, deseeded and finely diced
2 large eggs
2 teaspoons water
salt and pepper

Melt the margarine with the oil in an 18-cm/7-in omelette pan. Gently fry the onion until soft but not brown, about 5 minutes. Add the potato, tomato, mushrooms and finely diced pepper. Mix together and cook for 2 minutes. Lightly beat the eggs with the water, salt and pepper, pour over the vegetables and cook until the base is golden. Place under a moderate grill until the top is set and golden. Serve flat on a warm plate. SERVES 2.

Braised Red Cabbage

about 675 g/1½ lb shredded red cabbage, white pith removed
50 g/2 oz butter
1 medium onion, sliced
1 large cooking apple, peeled and sliced
150 ml/¼ pint light stock
2 teaspoons salt
1 tablespoon vinegar
½ teaspoon each powdered cloves and nutmeg
black pepper
1 tablespoon brown sugar

Place the cabbage in a large bowl and pour over boiling water
to cover. Leave for 1 minute then drain. This softens the
cabbage a little and makes it easier to pack into the saucepan.

Melt the butter in a heavy pan, add the onion and cook
gently for a few minutes to soften a little. Then add the apple,
stock, salt, vinegar, cloves, nutmeg and a good grinding of
black pepper. Add the cabbage, and turn it over well to mix
into the liquid. Cover tightly and cook gently until tender,
about 1½ hours, stirring through from time to time. Sprinkle
over the sugar at the end and serve with roast pork, ham or
any hot meal. SERVES 6.

If you wish, red wine can be substituted for the stock. This
dish heats up the following day with no loss of flavour.

Marrow and Onion Savoury

Illustrated on page 85

575–675 g/1¼–1½ lb marrow, peeled, deseeded, and cut into
small cubes
450 g/1 lb onions, finely sliced
dried mixed herbs
salt and pepper
25 g/1 oz butter
chopped parsley for garnish

Set the oven at 180 C, 350 F, gas 4.
Layer the marrow and onion in a greased ovenproof pie
dish, lightly sprinkling the mixed herbs and seasonings
between the layers, and ending with marrow. Dot the top
with the butter. Cover the dish – foil will do – and cook for
about 1½ hours until tender. Garnish with chopped parsley.
SERVES 4.
Marrow and Onion Savoury goes particularly well with
roast pork. It will cook quite happily in the lower part of the
oven under the meat.

Beetroot in White Sauce

6–8 small, even-sized beetroot, cooked, peeled, and kept hot
White sauce
25 g/1 oz margarine
25 g/1 oz flour
300 ml/½ pint milk
salt and pepper

To make the sauce, first melt the margarine in a small pan,
add the flour and cook, stirring for 1 minute. Stir in the milk,
and simmer for 1 minute. Add seasoning to taste, and pour
over the beetroot. SERVES 4.

Beetroot in Jelly

Illustrated opposite

1 kg/2 lb raw beetroot
½ (127-g/4½-oz) packet raspberry jelly
300 ml/½ pint white vinegar
6 cloves
6 peppercorns
1 small bay leaf

Wash the beetroot and trim away the leaves and most of the root, leaving 2.5 cm/1 in of the root still attached. (If the root is cut away too closely, the beetroot will 'bleed' during cooking.) Cook the beetroot in boiling water for 1½–2 hours until the skins will rub off easily but the beetroot still remain firm. Drain, rub off the skins with a damp cloth and cut the beetroot into 1-cm/½-in cubes. Pack the cubes into large jam jars.

Cut the jelly into pieces and put these into a heatproof jug or bowl. Mix the vinegar, cloves, peppercorns and bay leaf together in a pan, bring to the boil and simmer the mixture for 10 minutes. Strain the vinegar over the jelly, stirring until the jelly has dissolved completely. Allow to cool, then pour the liquid into the jam jars to cover the beetroot (if there is not quite enough liquid to do this, add a little more vinegar – there is no need to boil it first). Leave the jelly to set and cover the jars with non-metallic screw tops.

Beetroot in jelly is very good with cold roast lamb, beef, chicken and ham.

NOTE If you have no screw tops, melt a little paraffin wax (available from most chemists) and pour a thin layer over the set jelly to seal the beetroot. When the wax is firm, cover the jars with pieces of cellophane held in place with elastic bands.

Rice Salad with Stuffed Eggs (page 75), Marrow and Onion
Savoury (page 83) and Beetroot in Jelly (above)
Overleaf Minced Meat Plait (page 94) and Gooseberry
Butterscotch Pie (page 98)

Pastries and Pies

Savoury or sweet, served hot from the oven or chilled and eaten with cream, home-baked pies are much-loved favourites with everybody, young and old alike. They can be adapted to all seasons, too: while Steak and Kidney Pie makes a warming winter meal, Egg and Bacon Flan and Cornish Pasties can be taken on a picnic outdoors and, perhaps most satisfying of all, the apples or gooseberries from your own garden can be baked into a delightful fruit tart.

The secret of good shortcrust pastry, both savoury and sweet, is to handle it as little as possible while you are making it and rolling it out; this will ensure a light, crisp result. You will find that practice gives you a lighter touch and you will soon see signs of the progress you are making, as your creations take less and less time to disappear!

Shortcrust Pastry

175 g/6 oz plain flour
50 g/2 oz self-raising flour
pinch of salt
100 g/4 oz block margarine or 50 g/2 oz margarine and
50 g/2 oz lard
2–3 tablespoons water

Sift the flours and salt into a mixing bowl. Cut the fat into flakes and rub them into the flour. Gradually add enough water to bind the ingredients to a firm dough, roll this into a ball, wrap it in cooking foil or cling-film and chill it in the refrigerator for 15–30 minutes.

NOTE Shortcrust pastry can be made using all plain flour instead of part plain, part self-raising; but self-raising helps the pastry to brown more easily, making it crisp rather than hard in texture.

Cheese Pastry

225 g/8 oz plain flour
$\frac{1}{4}$ teaspoon salt
$\frac{1}{4}$ teaspoon mustard powder
pinch of cayenne
100 g/4 oz block margarine
75 g/3 oz Cheddar cheese, finely grated
1 egg yolk
2–3 tablespoons water

Sift the flour into a mixing bowl with the salt, mustard and cayenne. Cut the margarine into flakes and rub them into the dry ingredients. Stir in the cheese and mix everything to a firm dough with the egg yolk and water. Roll the dough into a ball, wrap it in cling-film or kitchen foil and chill it in the refrigerator for 15–30 minutes.

Sweet Flan Pastry

Makes 175 g/6 oz, enough to line an 18-cm/7-in or a 20-cm/8-in flan ring or tin

175 g/6 oz plain flour
pinch of salt
75 g/3 oz block margarine
1 tablespoon caster sugar
2 teaspoons cold water
1 egg yolk

Mix the flour and salt together in a bowl. Cut the margarine into flakes and rub them into the flour. In a separate bowl or a cup, dissolve the sugar in the water and stir in the egg yolk. Add these ingredients to the flour and mix everything together to a firm dough. Add a little more water if necessary, but be careful not to make the dough too wet. Roll the dough into a ball, wrap it in cling-film or kitchen foil and chill it in the refrigerator for 30 minutes.

Lining a Flan Ring

Place an 18-cm/7-in or a 20-cm/8-in flan ring on a baking sheet which has a flat edge; this will make removing the cooked pastry case easier. (If you have a flan tin or dish rather than a ring you do not of course need a baking sheet at all.) On a floured board roll out one quantity of shortcrust, sweet shortcrust or cheese pastry to a round about 5 cm/2 in larger in diameter than the flan ring and lift it carefully into the ring, taking care that you do not tear it. Press the pastry gently into the side and base of the ring, making sure that there are no air bubbles between the pastry and the tray. Trim away any surplus pastry from the edge of the ring and roll across the top with a rolling pin to smooth.

Baking Blind

To bake 'blind' means to bake a pastry case before you put in the filling. This is not always necessary, but it's a good idea if you want to ensure that the bottom of a flan or quiche is thoroughly cooked.

Prick the base of the pastry case all over with a fork. Cut out a round of greaseproof paper 6 cm/2½ in larger in diameter than the flan ring and grease it lightly. Fit it into the pastry case, greased side down, and cover it to a depth of 1 cm/½ in with dried peas or haricot beans; their weight will prevent the pastry from rising. Bake the pastry case in a moderately hot oven (200 C, 400 F, gas 6) for 15 minutes, then remove the beans and the paper and bake for a further 10–15 minutes. The case is now ready for you to add the filling.

Allow the dried peas or beans to cool and store them in a screw-topped jar; they can be used over and over again.

Steak and Kidney Pie

Filling
575 g/1¼ lb lean pie beef or stewing steak
100 g/4 oz ox kidney
1 tablespoon plain flour
¾ teaspoon salt
¼ teaspoon pepper
100 g/4 oz onion
2 tablespoons beef dripping or oil
2 teaspoons Worcestershire sauce
300 ml/½ pint water
Pastry
225 g/8 oz self-raising flour
½ teaspoon salt
50 g/2 oz block margarine
50 g/2 oz lard
2–3 tablespoons water
beaten egg to glaze

Cut the steak into 2.5-cm/1-in chunks and the kidney into slightly smaller pieces. Sift the flour with the salt and pepper and coat the pieces of meat well with the mixture. Chop the onion. Heat the dripping or oil in a pan, add the onion and meat and fry for about 2–3 minutes, until all the pieces of meat are sealed. Pour in the Worcestershire sauce and the water and bring to the boil, stirring continuously. Cover the pan and simmer the meat for 1¾–2 hours, until tender. Stir from time to time to prevent the meat from sticking to the bottom of the pan.

Meanwhile, make the pastry. Mix the flour and salt together in a mixing bowl, cut the margarine and lard into flakes and rub them into the dry ingredients. Add enough water to make a firm but pliable dough, wrap it in cooking foil and chill it in the refrigerator for 30 minutes.

On a lightly floured surface, roll the pastry out to fit the top of a 900-ml/1½-pint pie dish, but making it 2.5 cm/1 in larger all round. Strain the gravy from the cooked meat into a basin or a jug and put the meat itself into the pie dish. Add 3–4 tablespoons of the gravy. Cut a 1.5-cm/¾-in border from the pastry shape, dampen the rim of the pie dish and arrange the pastry strip all the way round, pressing down well. Now moisten the upper side of the pastry strip and place the remaining pastry shape on the pie, pressing the edges together with your finger and thumb to make a fluted pattern. Brush the top of the pie with beaten egg. Roll out any remaining pastry and use it to cut out leaves and other decorations for the top of the pie. Place these on the pie and brush them with more beaten egg.

Bake the pie in a hot oven (220C, 425F, gas 7) for 15–20 minutes to set the pastry, then lower the heat to moderately hot (190C, 375F, gas 5) for a further 20 minutes. Heat the reserved gravy in a pan and serve it in a sauce boat with the pie. SERVES 4–6.

Chicken Pie

1 (370-g/13-oz) packet frozen puff pastry
350 g/12 oz cooked chicken
1 small onion
giblets and wing tips from the chicken
1 small bay leaf
8–9 peppercorns
600 ml/1 pint water
100 g/4 oz mushrooms (optional)
40 g/1½ oz margarine
40 g/1½ oz plain flour
salt and pepper
beaten egg to glaze

Allow the pastry to thaw at room temperature following the instructions on the packet. Cut the chicken into bite-size pieces and leave these on one side.

Slice the onion. Wash the giblets in cold water and place them in a pan with the wing tips, onion, bay leaf, peppercorns and water. Cover the pan, bring to the boil and simmer the stock for 1 hour. Strain the stock, return it to the rinsed out pan, bring it once more to the boil and boil it hard until it is reduced to 450 ml/¾ pint in volume.

Clean, trim and slice the mushrooms, if used. Melt the margarine in a pan, stir in the flour and allow to cook for 1 minute. Gradually stir in the stock, bring the sauce to the boil and boil it for 2 minutes, stirring continuously. Season to taste with salt and pepper and mix in the mushrooms followed by the chicken.

On a lightly floured surface, roll the puff pastry out to cover a 1.15-litre/2-pint pie dish as for Steak and Kidney Pie (page 90). Pour the chicken mixture into the dish and top with the pastry. Brush the pie with beaten egg and bake it in a hot oven (220C, 425F, gas 7) for 20 minutes, then lower the heat to moderately hot (190C, 375F, gas 5) for a further 20–25 minutes, until the pastry is well-risen and golden brown. SERVES 4.

Cornish Pasties

A true Cornish pasty should be made with uncooked, good beef steak. Using minced beef or even left-over cooked meat as I do is breaking with tradition, but it does make for a cheaper, faster-cooking pasty!

225 g/8 oz roughly minced beef or cooked beef cut into small pieces
1 tablespoon stock or water
225 g/8 oz finely chopped vegetables (potatoes, onions, carrots)
½ teaspoon salt
¼ teaspoon pepper
225 g/8 oz Shortcrust Pastry (page 88)
beaten egg to glaze

Moisten the meat with the stock or water and mix in the vegetables, salt and pepper. Roll the pastry out on a lightly floured surface and cut out seven or eight 13-cm/5-in rounds, using a plain pastry cutter or a saucer. Spoon a little of the meat mixture down the centre of each round. Dampen the edges of the pastry on either side of the meat with a little water and bring them up over the filling, joining them in the centre in the traditional Cornish pasty shape. Press the edges together in a fluting pattern with your finger and thumb. Arrange the pasties on a baking sheet, brush them with beaten egg and bake them in a moderately hot oven (200 C, 400 F, gas 6) for 35 minutes. Lower the heat slightly during cooking if they are browning too quickly. SERVES 4–6.

Minced Meat Plait

Illustrated on page 86

1 (212-g/7½-oz) packet frozen puff pastry
225 g/8 oz sausagemeat or any minced, cooked meat (chicken
and boiled ham are especially good)
1 tablespoon tomato ketchup
1 teaspoon chopped fresh parsley or ½ teaspoon dried mixed
herbs
¼ teaspoon salt
generous pinch of pepper
2 tomatoes
beaten egg to glaze

Allow the pastry to thaw at room temperature, following the instructions on the packet.

Mix together the minced meat, tomato ketchup, herbs, salt and pepper. Cut crosses in the bases of the tomatoes, plunge them briefly into boiling water, then into cold water and peel away the skins. Slice the tomatoes and leave them on one side.

On a lightly floured surface, roll the pastry out to a rectangle measuring approximately 25 × 20 cm/10 × 8 in and trim the edges neatly. Mark the rectangle lengthways into thirds and arrange the meat filling down the centre third of the pastry, leaving a 1-cm/½-in gap at the top and bottom. Top the filling with the sliced tomatoes. Brush the surface of the rest of the rectangle with water and make diagonal cuts on either side of the filling at 2.5-cm/1-in intervals, stopping just short of the filling. Beginning at the top of the rectangle, fold these 2.5-cm/1-in strips alternately over each other, covering the meat in a plait pattern. Pinch together the pastry edges at the top and bottom of the plait to seal and leave the plait to rest on one side for 30 minutes, if possible. Then brush it with beaten egg and bake it in a hot oven (220 C, 425 F, gas 7) for 15 minutes before lowering the heat to moderately hot (190 C, 375 F, gas 5) and continuing baking for a further 15–20 minutes, until the pastry is well-risen and golden.

Minced meat plait can be eaten hot or cold. SERVES 4.

Sausage Whirls

225 g/8 oz self-raising flour
¾ teaspoon salt
50 g/2 oz block margarine
50 g/2 oz grated Cheddar cheese
6–7 tablespoons milk
a little yeast extract
225 g/8 oz sausagemeat
1½ tablespoons tomato ketchup
1 egg, beaten
generous sprinkling of black pepper
pinch of dried mixed herbs

Mix the flour in a bowl with ¼ teaspoon of the salt. Cut the margarine into flakes and rub them into the flour. Stir in the cheese and add enough milk to bind all the ingredients to a firm dough. Roll the dough out on a lightly floured surface to a 35.5 × 23-cm/14 × 9-in rectangle and spread this thinly with yeast extract.

Mix the sausagemeat with the tomato ketchup, beaten egg, remaining salt, the pepper and herbs until all the ingredients are thoroughly combined and spread the filling on the pastry rectangle to within 1 cm/½ in of the edges. Roll up the pastry lengthways like a Swiss roll and cut the roll into slices about 8 mm/⅜ in thick. Arrange the sausage whirls on a lightly greased baking sheet and bake them in a hot oven (220 C, 425 F, gas 7) for 15 minutes, until golden brown. Leave them to cool on a wire rack. SERVES 4.

Yorkshire Egg and Bacon Flan

175 g/6 oz shortcrust or cheese pastry (page 88)
100 g/4 oz streaky bacon
1 onion
2 eggs
175 ml/6 fl oz top of the milk
$\frac{3}{4}$ teaspoon salt
$\frac{1}{4}$ teaspoon pepper
75 g/3 oz Cheddar cheese, grated

Use the pastry to line a 20-cm/8-in flan tin or a flan ring placed on a baking sheet (see page 89). Set the oven at hot (220 C, 425 F, gas 7) and, if you are using a flan tin, place a baking sheet in the oven to heat up.

Remove the rind from the bacon and cut the rashers into small pieces. Finely chop the onion. Dry-fry the bacon gently for a few minutes until the fat runs, then transfer it to a plate. Fry the onion in the bacon fat until soft but not browned and spread it over the base of the flan with the bacon. Lightly beat the eggs and stir in the milk, salt and pepper. Sprinkle half the grated cheese into the flan, pour in the egg and milk mixture and scatter the remaining cheese over the top. Bake the flan on the hot baking sheet for 20 minutes (the baking sheet ensures that the pastry base is thoroughly cooked as well as the filling), then reduce the oven temperature to moderately hot (200 C, 400 F, gas 6) and continue baking for a further 10–15 minutes until the flan is set and golden on top.

Serve hot or cold with a crisp green salad. SERVES 4–6.

Variation

For a richer flan, use single cream instead of top of the milk.

Crunchy Apple Tart

450 g/1 lb cooking apples
25 g/1 oz butter
75 g/3 oz granulated sugar
175 g/6 oz plain flour
pinch of salt
25 g/1 oz caster sugar
75 g/3 oz block margarine
50 g/2 oz raisins
25 g/1 oz desiccated coconut

Peel, core and thinly slice the cooking apples. Melt the butter in a pan, add the apple and cook gently over a low heat, stirring occasionally, for 10–15 minutes, until the apple is beginning to soften. Mix in 50 g/2 oz of the granulated sugar.

Combine the flour, salt and caster sugar in a bowl. Cut the margarine into flakes and rub them into the dry ingredients until the mixture resembles fine breadcrumbs. Lightly grease an 18-cm/7-in flan tin or a flan ring placed on a greased baking tray and sprinkle the base with two-thirds of the flour mixture. Bake in a moderate oven (180 C, 350 F, gas 4) for 15 minutes.

Stir the raisins into the cooked apple and spread the filling over the crumble base to within 1 cm/½ in of the edge. Mix the coconut and the rest of the granulated sugar into the remaining uncooked crumble mixture and sprinkle the crumble over the apple, covering it right to the edge of the flan tin or ring. Return the tart to the oven and bake it for a further 15–20 minutes, until golden. Eat it warm with single cream. SERVES 4–6.

Gooseberry Butterscotch Pie

Illustrated on page 86

450 g/1 lb dessert gooseberries
1 (18-cm/7-in) sweet flan pastry case,
baked blind (pages 89–90)
50 g/2 oz plain flour
25 g/1 oz light soft brown sugar
2 tablespoons golden syrup
1 egg, beaten
6 tablespoons milk

Top and tail the gooseberries and arrange them in the pastry case. Mix the flour with the sugar, golden syrup, beaten egg and milk and beat all the ingredients thoroughly together to combine. Spread the mixture over the gooseberries and bake the pie in a moderately hot oven (190 C, 375 F, gas 5) for about 30 minutes, until the filling is set and golden. Serve hot or cold with whipped cream. SERVES 4–6.

Sweet Mint Pasties

225 g/8 oz shortcrust pastry (page 88)
25 g/1 oz butter
2 tablespoons finely chopped fresh mint
100 g/4 oz currants
50 g/2 oz light soft brown sugar
grated rind of a small lemon
a little milk to glaze
caster sugar for sprinkling

Roll the pastry out on a lightly floured surface and cut out five or six 15-cm/6-in rounds, using a plain pastry cutter or a tea plate. Melt the butter and mix it with the mint, currants, brown sugar and lemon rind. Place some of the mixture on one half of each pastry round, dampen the edges of the pastry and fold the other half over the filling. Seal the edges, pressing them together in a crimping pattern with your finger and thumb.

Arrange the pasties on a baking sheet, brush them with milk and sprinkle them with a little caster sugar. Bake them in a moderately hot oven (200 C, 400 F, gas 6) for about 20 minutes, until golden. SERVES 5–6.

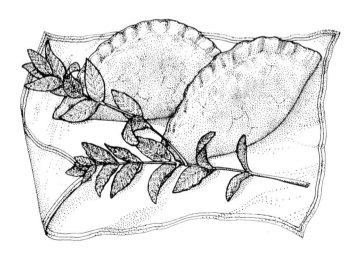

Apricot Sandwich

100 g/4 oz butter or block margarine
225 g/8 oz self-raising flour
100 g/4 oz soft brown sugar
1 egg, beaten
½ teaspoon vanilla essence
1 tablespoon milk
3 tablespoons apricot jam
icing sugar for sprinkling

Grease an 18-cm/7-in or a 20-cm/8-in sponge sandwich tin or a flan ring placed on a baking tray.

Cut the butter or margarine into flakes. Put the flour into a mixing bowl, rub in the fat and stir in the sugar. Add the beaten egg, the vanilla and milk and mix all the ingredients to a firm dough. Divide the dough into two portions and roll each out on a lightly floured surface to fit the flan tin or ring. Place one pastry round in the tin and spread it with jam to within 1 cm/½ in of the edge. Cover with the second round.

Bake the Apricot Sandwich in a moderate oven (180 C, 350 F, gas 4) for about ¾–1 hour. Leave it to cool in the tin for 10–15 minutes, then turn it out on to a wire rack. Sprinkle it with icing sugar before serving. SERVES 6.

Hot and Cold Puddings

'What's for pudding?' is the cry that goes up in many a household, often before the main course has even been served. Children love puddings – hot and cold, creams, crumbles, mousses and fools – and so do most adults. Here is a collection of all our favourite puddings, ranging from warming, substantial ones like Orange Suet Pudding and Hot Blackberry and Apple Trifle, to be served on a cold day after a lighter main course, to special party treats such as Chocolate Orange Mousse.

No main meal ever seems *quite* complete without a pudding and when we have such a lovely range of traditional, nourishing recipes to choose from, it seems a shame not to make full use of them.

Orange Suet Pudding

100 g/4 oz self-raising flour
50 g/2 oz shredded suet
50 g/2 oz caster sugar
grated rind and juice of 2 oranges
50 g/2 oz sultanas (optional)
2 tablespoons golden syrup

Sift the flour into a mixing bowl and combine it with the suet, sugar, orange rind and sultanas, if used. Gradually stir in enough orange juice to bind the mixture to a fairly stiff consistency. Grease a 900-ml/1½-pint pudding basin and put the mixture inside. Cover the surface with a piece of greased greaseproof paper, making a 2.5-cm/1-in pleat down the centre of the paper to allow the pudding to expand. Seal the basin with a piece of cooking foil, pressing the foil round the rim of the basin and securing it with string. Stand the basin in a steamer and place this inside a large saucepan of boiling water; the water should reach two-thirds way up the basin. Steam the pudding for 2 hours, topping up the boiling water when necessary.

To make the sauce, pour the remaining orange juice into a small pan and add the syrup. Bring the mixture to boiling point, stirring, and transfer it to a sauce boat. Turn the pudding out on to a warm plate and serve it with the orange sauce and custard, if liked. SERVES 4.

Pineapple Upside-down pudding (page 106) and Pears in
Chocolate Sauce (page 111)
Overleaf, from the back Dundee Cake (page 117), Almond
Slices (page 124), Crunchy Biscuits (page 126) and
Wholewheat Gingerbread (page 120)

Apple Charlotte

It is difficult to give exact quantities for this pudding as they will depend on the size of the dish you use.

675 g–1 kg/1½–2 lb cooking apples
a little water
3–4 tablespoons sugar · stale white bread
50–75 g/2–3 oz sponge cake crumbs
grated rind and juice of half a lemon
Sauce
2 tablespoons apricot jam
1 tablespoon water · 1 tablespoon lemon juice

Peel, core and thinly slice the apples and put them in a pan with just enough water to cover the bottom. Cook them over a low heat, stirring occasionally, for 20–25 minutes, until reduced to a purée. Add more water during cooking if necessary. Sweeten to taste with the sugar.

Butter a charlotte mould or a soufflé dish. Remove the crust from the bread and cut it into 5 mm/¼ in-thick slices. Trim a round of bread or cut several pieces to a shape to fit snugly into the bottom of the dish and place them inside. Keep a few slices of bread on one side for later use and butter the rest. Slice them into strips 5 cm/2 in wide and arrange them, overlapping slightly, round the inside edge of the dish, butter-side facing inwards. Stir the cake crumbs and the lemon rind and juice into the apple purée to make a stiff mixture and spoon the mixture into the dish. Cut the reserved pieces of bread to fit tightly into the dish on top of the apple and place them in position. Bake the pudding in a moderately hot oven (190 C, 375 F, gas 5) for about 40 minutes. If you find it is browning too quickly, cover the top with a piece of cooking foil. Turn the charlotte upside down on to a warm serving dish but leave the dish in place for 10 minutes.

To make the sauce, warm the apricot jam, the water and lemon juice together in a pan. Lift away the charlotte mould or dish and brush all sides of the pudding well with the sauce. Serve hot with custard or single cream. SERVES 6.

Pineapple Upside-
down Pudding

Illustrated on page 103

40g/1½oz butter
75g/5oz demerara sugar
6 canned pineapple rings
a few glacé cherries, halved
75g/3oz soft margarine
75g/3oz caster sugar
1 large egg, beaten
100g/4oz self-raising flour
25g/1oz semolina
2–3 tablespoons milk
1½ teaspoons arrowroot
200ml/7floz pineapple juice

Spread the butter thickly over the bottom and side of a 20-cm/8-in sandwich tin. Sprinkle in the demerara sugar. Arrange the pineapple rings and glacé cherries in a pattern in the bottom of the tin.

Beat the margarine, caster sugar, egg, flour and semolina together in a bowl until smooth and add enough milk to give the mixture a soft, dropping consistency. Spread it carefully over the fruit and bake the pudding in a moderately hot oven (190C, 375F, gas 5) for 30–35 minutes, until the top is firm. Take it out of the oven and turn it upside down on to a warm plate, leaving the tin in position.

To make the sauce, whisk the arrowroot into the pineapple juice and heat the mixture gently in a pan. Bring to the boil, stirring continuously, and boil for about 1 minute, until it has become clear. Remove the tin from the pudding, spoon a little of the sauce over the pineapple for a glaze and serve the rest in a jug alongside. SERVES 6.

Oat and Apple Crumble

450 g/1 lb dessert apples
2 tablespoons mincemeat, raspberry or strawberry jam or
marmalade
1 tablespoon granulated sugar · 1 tablespoon water
75 g/3 oz plain flour · pinch of salt
50 g/2 oz block margarine · 50 g/2 oz rolled oats
3 tablespoons demerara sugar
a little grated nutmeg

Peel, core and thinly slice the apples. Spread the mincemeat, jam or marmalade in the bottom of a 1.15-litre/2-pint ovenproof dish and arrange the apple on top. Sprinkle in the granulated sugar and the water.

Mix the flour and salt together in a bowl. Cut the margarine into flakes and rub them into the flour until the mixture resembles fine breadcrumbs. Stir in the oats followed by 2 tablespoons of the demerara sugar and sprinkle the crumble over the apple. Scatter the remaining sugar on top with the grated nutmeg and bake the crumble in a moderate oven (180 C, 350 F, gas 4) for 1 hour or alternatively in a moderately hot oven (190 C, 375 F, gas 5) for 45 minutes. Serve hot with custard. SERVES 4.

Baked Custard

450 ml/¾ pint milk
1 tablespoon sugar
3 eggs and 1 egg yolk
a little grated nutmeg

Warm the milk gently in a pan with the sugar, stirring until the sugar has dissolved. Do not allow to boil. Beat together the eggs and egg yolk, pour in the hot milk and transfer the mixture to an ovenproof dish. Sprinkle the top with a little grated nutmeg and stand the dish in a small roasting tin containing enough warm water to come half-way up the side of the dish. Bake the custard in a moderate oven (160 C, 325 F, gas 3) for about 1 hour, until firm. Test this by inserting a skewer into the custard: if it comes out clean, the dish is ready. SERVES 4.

Country Fruit Bake

100 g/4 oz dried apricots
100 g/4 oz prunes
1 large banana
3 tablespoons honey
150 ml/¼ pint sweet cider
finely grated rind of 1 orange and 1 lemon
50 g/2 oz butter, cut into flakes

Put the apricots and prunes into separate bowls, cover with boiling water and leave to soak for 1 hour. Drain them.
  Butter a shallow ovenproof dish. Cut the banana into 2.5 cm/1 in-thick slices, arrange them in the bottom of the dish and cover them with the apricots and prunes. Dissolve the honey in the cider and pour the liquid over the fruit. Sprinkle the top with orange and lemon rind, dot with the butter and bake, uncovered, in a cool oven (150 C, 300 F, gas 2) for 1½–2 hours, until the fruit is glazed and tender. Stir it occasionally while it is baking. SERVES 4.

Hot Apple and Blackberry Trifle

450 g/1 lb cooking apples
2 tablespoons water
50 g/2 oz granulated sugar
225 g/½ lb blackberries
1 Swiss roll
2 large eggs
1 tablespoon cornflour
300 ml/½ pint milk
½ teaspoon vanilla essence
100 g/4 oz caster sugar
a little caster sugar for sprinkling

Peel, core and thickly slice the apples and put them in a pan with the water and half the granulated sugar. Cook them gently over a low heat for about 15 minutes, until just tender. Carefully stir in the blackberries.

Set the oven at moderate (160 C, 325 F, gas 3). Cut the Swiss roll into nine slices and arrange these around the side of a 1.75-litre/3-pint soufflé or other ovenproof dish. Spoon the fruit into the centre.

Separate the eggs. Beat the yolks and mix in the cornflour. Heat the milk and the remaining granulated sugar together in a pan until the sugar has dissolved and pour the liquid into the egg yolk mixture. Combine all the ingredients, return the custard to the pan and heat it slowly to just below boiling point, stirring continuously. Allow it to cool slightly and stir in the vanilla. Pour the custard over the fruit, spreading it level with a spoon.

Whisk the egg whites until stiff and sprinkle in half the caster sugar. Whisk them again until very stiff and fold in all the rest of the sugar. Spoon the meringue over the custard, roughing the surface into peaks with a fork, and sprinkle the top with a little more caster sugar. Bake at once in the oven for 20 minutes or until golden. Serve hot. SERVES 6.

Baked Floating Islands

4 eggs
175 g/6 oz caster sugar
600 ml/1 pint milk
½ teaspoon vanilla essence

Set the oven at cool (150 C, 300 F, gas 2). Butter a shallow, 1.15-litre/2-pint ovenproof dish and stand it on a baking sheet.

Separate two of the eggs and put the whites into a clean, dry bowl. Place the yolks in a separate bowl with the remaining eggs and 50 g/2 oz of the sugar and beat lightly to combine. Heat the milk and vanilla in a pan until hot but not boiling and pour the mixture into the egg yolks, beating well. Transfer the custard to the ovenproof dish.

Whisk the egg whites until stiff and sprinkle in half the remaining sugar. Whisk again until the whites are very stiff and fold in all the rest of the sugar. Arrange the meringue in tablespoonfuls on the custard and bake at once in the oven for about 45 minutes, until the custard is set. If the meringues are browning too quickly, reduce the heat a little. SERVES 4.

Pears in Chocolate Sauce

Illustrated on page 103

1 (410-g/14½-oz) can pear halves
1 packet of 16 sponge fingers
Chocolate sauce
100 g/4 oz plain dessert chocolate
1 tablespoon rum
50 g/2 oz caster sugar
1 teaspoon arrowroot
2 egg yolks, beaten
300 ml/½ pint milk
1 (142-ml/5-fl oz) carton double cream
25 g/1 oz chopped nuts to decorate

Drain the pears, reserving the juice. Lay the sponge fingers in a row in a long, narrow serving dish and spoon over some of the pear syrup to soften them. Place the pears on top.

To make the sauce, break up the chocolate and put the pieces into a basin with the rum. Stand the basin over a pan of very hot, not boiling water, making sure that the water does not touch the basin, and allow the chocolate to melt gently, stirring occasionally.

Mix the sugar and arrowroot into the egg yolks and stir in a little of the milk to blend. Pour in the rest of the milk followed by the chocolate, transfer the sauce to a pan and stir it over a gentle heat until it thickens just enough to coat the back of a spoon. Do not allow it to boil or it may curdle.

Leave the sauce to cool and spoon it over the pears. Whip the cream until stiff, put it inside a piping bag fitted with a large star-shaped nozzle and pipe rosettes on top of the pears. Or, simply arrange the cream in spoonfuls on them. Decorate with chopped nuts and serve. SERVES 4.

Creamy Coffee Mould

2 eggs
25 g/1 oz cornflour
75 g/3 oz caster sugar
1 tablespoon instant coffee powder
1 tablespoon drinking chocolate powder
450 ml/¾ pint milk
15 g/½ oz gelatine
3 tablespoons water
1 (170-g/6-oz) can evaporated milk or 1 (142-ml/5-fl oz)
carton whipping cream

Lightly oil a 1.15-litre/2-pint pudding mould.

Separate the eggs. Mix the yolks in a basin with the cornflour, sugar, the coffee and chocolate powder and a little of the milk. Heat the rest of the milk in a pan and pour it gradually into the mixture, stirring well to combine. Transfer the mixture to a pan and heat it gently to just below boiling point, stirring as it thickens. Remove the pan from the heat.

Soften the gelatine in the water; it will set into a cake. Add this to the hot coffee mixture and stir until it has thoroughly dissolved. Whip the evaporated milk or the cream until thick and fold it into the mixture. Whisk the egg whites until stiff but not dry and fold these in too. Pour the pudding into the oiled mould and leave it to set in a cool place for 3–4 hours.

To serve, dip the mould briefly into hot water and turn the pudding out on to a plate. SERVES 6.

Chocolate Orange Mousse

175 g/6 oz plain dessert chocolate
2 tablespoons fresh orange juice
20 g/¾ oz butter
1 teaspoon grated orange rind
3 eggs
chopped nuts and whipped cream to decorate (optional)

Break up the chocolate and put the pieces in a basin with the orange juice. Stand the basin over a pan of hot, not boiling water, making sure the water does not touch the basin, and melt the chocolate gently, stirring occasionally to combine it with the orange juice. Remove the basin from the heat and beat in the butter and orange rind.

Separate the eggs. Beat the yolks into the chocolate mixture and leave until cool but not beginning to set. Whisk the egg whites until stiff but not dry and fold them into the mixture. Pour the mousse into a serving dish or into individual bowls and chill it in the refrigerator. Serve decorated with chopped nuts and whipped cream, if liked. SERVES 4.

Pineapple Delight

1 (425-g/15-oz) can pineapple rings
2 eggs
3 tablespoons plus 2 teaspoons caster sugar
grated rind and juice of 1 small lemon
15 g/$\frac{1}{2}$ oz gelatine
1 (170-g/6-oz) can evaporated milk

Drain the pineapple, reserving the juice, and wipe the slices dry. Keep 2–3 rings on one side for decoration and finely chop the rest.

Separate the eggs. Whisk the yolks, 3 tablespoons caster sugar, the lemon rind and the gelatine together in a small pan and stir in 150 ml/$\frac{1}{4}$ pint pineapple juice and 3 tablespoons of the lemon juice. Heat the mixture gently, stirring until the gelatine has dissolved; do not allow it to boil. Pour the mixture into a bowl. Add the chopped pineapple and leave to cool until the mixture is just beginning to set.

Meanwhile, whip the evaporated milk with the rest of the lemon juice until it thickens. Whisk the egg whites until stiff but not dry and whisk in the remaining sugar. Fold the milk first into the setting pineapple mixture, then the egg white and pour the pudding into a glass serving bowl. Cut the reserved pineapple rings into pieces. Arrange these on top of the pudding to decorate and leave it in a cool place to set completely. SERVES 4–6.

Cakes and Biscuits

The smell of a freshly baked cake drifting out of a warm kitchen is often one of the earliest things we remember, as well as being one of the most delicious and enticing.

There are three basic methods of cake making: rubbing in, when the fat is rubbed into the flour as in making pastry – this is used for the plainer types of cake; creaming, when the fat and sugar are beaten together until the mixture looks like stiffly whipped cream, probably the most common way of making cakes; and melting fat, when the fat is melted before being added to the dry ingredients, a method used for gingerbreads and some kinds of fruit cakes.

You will be able to tell when a cake is done as it should be shrinking away from the sides of the tin. A sponge cake will be well risen and springy to the touch, while a skewer inserted right through the centre of a fruit cake should come out perfectly clean. Biscuits must never be overcooked but baked until just golden, then taken out of the oven and allowed to stand on the baking sheet for a few minutes until they begin to go crisp. They should then be cooled completely on a wire rack and stored in an airtight tin.

Nutty Fruit Cake

150 g/5 oz margarine
6 tablespoons golden syrup
175 g/6 oz raisins or sultanas
175 g/6 oz currants
50 g/2 oz chopped dried apricots
50 g/2 oz candied peel
50 g/2 oz blanched chopped almonds
8 tablespoons milk
225 g/8 oz plain flour
pinch of salt
1 teaspoon mixed spice
1 teaspoon cinnamon
2 eggs, beaten
½ teaspoon bicarbonate of soda

Set the oven at cool (150 C, 300 F, gas 2). Grease an 18-cm/7-in square cake tin and line it with greased greaseproof paper. Put the margarine, syrup, fruit, candied peel, nuts and milk together in a pan and heat gently until the fat has melted. Simmer the mixture over a low heat for 5 minutes and allow to cool.

Sift the flour, salt and spices into a large mixing bowl. Stir in the beaten egg. Sprinkle the bicarbonate of soda into the cooled fruit and nut mixture, stir quickly to disperse it and pour the mixture into the dry ingredients. Combine everything thoroughly. Transfer the mixture to the cake tin and bake it for 1¼–2 hours, until the top is firm and the cake is beginning to shrink away from the sides of the tin. Allow it to stand for 10–15 minutes, then turn it out on to a wire rack and leave it to cool completely.

Dundee Cake

Illustrated on page 104

175 g/6 oz butter or margarine, softened
175 g/6 oz caster sugar
½ teaspoon almond essense
200 g/7 oz self-raising flour
25 g/1 oz ground almonds
100 g/4 oz sultanas
100 g/4 oz raisins
100 g/4 oz currants
50 g/2 oz glacé cherries, halved
50 g/2 oz candied peel
3 eggs, beaten
40–50 g/1½–2 oz almonds, split in half

Grease and line an 18-cm/7-in square or a 20-cm/8-in round cake tin, brushing the paper well with melted butter or oil. Set the oven at moderate (160 C, 325 F, gas 3).

Beat together the fat, sugar and almond essence until light and fluffy. Mix the flour in a separate bowl with the ground almonds, the dried fruit, the cherries and peel. Gradually beat the egg into the fat and sugar mixture, alternating with spoonfuls of the mixed fruit and flour. When all the ingredients are thoroughly combined, turn the mixture into the cake tin, arrange the halved almonds neatly over the surface, rounded side up, pressing them in lightly and bake the cake in the preheated oven for 1¾ hours or until a skewer inserted in the centre comes out clean. Leave it to cool in the tin for about 1 hour before turning it out on to a wire rack.

This cake will keep well for several weeks if wrapped in aluminium foil.

Malt Loaf

225 g/8 oz self-raising flour
½ teaspoon salt
½ teaspoon bicarbonate of soda
75 g/3 oz sultanas
75 g/3 oz malt extract
75 g/3 oz black treacle
150 ml/¼ pint milk
1 egg, beaten

Set the oven at moderate (180 C, 350 F, gas 4). Grease a 1-kg/2-lb loaf tin and line the base with a piece of greased greaseproof paper.

Sift the flour, salt and bicarbonate of soda into a large mixing bowl and stir in the sultanas. Warm the malt and treacle gently together in a pan until they have become liquid and stir in the milk and beaten egg. Pour the mixture into the dry ingredients and beat gently until everything is thoroughly combined.

Transfer the mixture to the loaf tin and bake it in the oven for 30 minutes. Reduce the heat slightly to 160 C, 325 F, gas 3, if the loaf seems to be browning too quickly and continue cooking for a further 15–20 minutes, until it is springy to the touch and beginning to come away from the sides of the tin. Leave it to cool in the tin for 10 minutes before turning it out on to a wire rack.

Malt loaf is delicious served sliced and buttered.

Date and Walnut Loaf

50 g/2 oz margarine
225 g/8 oz chopped dates
50 g/2 oz caster sugar
pinch of salt
1 teaspoon bicarbonate of soda
150 ml/$\frac{1}{4}$ pint boiling water
50 g/2 oz chopped walnuts
1 egg, beaten
225 g/8 oz self-raising flour
$\frac{1}{2}$ teaspoon vanilla essence

Set the oven at moderate (160 C, 325 F, gas 3). Grease and line a 1-kg/2-lb loaf tin, brushing the paper well with melted butter or oil.

Put the margarine, dates, sugar, salt and bicarbonate of soda together in a bowl and pour over the boiling water. Allow the mixture to cool a little, stirring to help the margarine to melt. Add the walnuts, beaten egg, flour and vanilla and mix all the ingredients well together. Pour the mixture into the loaf tin and bake it for 1$\frac{1}{4}$–1$\frac{1}{2}$ hours, until firm to the touch and beginning to shrink away from the sides of the tin.

Leave the loaf in the tin for 10-15 minutes, then turn it out on to a wire rack.

Wholewheat Gingerbread

Illustrated on page 104

75 g/3 oz plain flour
pinch of salt
½ teaspoon cinnamon
3 teaspoons ground ginger
1 teaspoon bicarbonate of soda
150 g/5 oz wholewheat flour
40 g/1½ oz demerara sugar
50 g/2 oz sultanas
25 g/1 oz candied peel
100 g/4 oz margarine
100 g/4 oz golden syrup
100 g/4 oz black treacle
1 large egg, beaten
150 ml/¼ pint milk

Set the oven at cool (150 C, 300 F, gas 2). Grease and line an 18-cm/7-in square cake tin, brushing the paper well with melted butter or oil.

Sift the plain flour, the salt, spices and bicarbonate of soda into a large mixing bowl. Add the wholewheat flour, the sugar, sultanas and candied peel. Put the margarine in a pan with the syrup and treacle and heat gently until the margarine has melted. Take the pan off the heat, stir in the beaten egg and the milk and pour the mixture into the dry ingredients. Mix everything well together, transfer the mixture to the cake tin and bake it for about 1 hour, until firm and springy to the touch.

Leave the gingerbread to cool in the tin and store it for a few days before cutting to allow the flavour to develop.

Fudge Cakes

100 g/4 oz self-raising flour
50 g/2 oz margarine
50 g/2 oz soft brown sugar
1 egg, beaten
1–2 tablespoons milk
Filling
15 g/½ oz margarine
15 g/½ oz soft brown sugar

Set the oven at moderately hot (190 C, 375 F, gas 5). Grease 12 patty tins.

Put the flour into a mixing bowl and rub in the margarine. Add the sugar, the beaten egg and just enough milk to give a stiff dropping consistency. Divide the mixture into three portions: leave one portion on one side and put a little of the rest into each patty tin, filling it to half way. Make a dent in the centre of each bun with a damp teaspoon.

To make the filling, cream the margarine with the sugar until fluffy and divide the mixture between the patty tins, spooning a little into the dent in each bun. Cover with the remaining portion of cake mixture and bake in the preheated oven for 15–17 minutes.

West Riding Moggie

Here are two quite different versions of West Riding Moggie, each one claiming to be authentic. As they are so good, I have included them both.

Light Moggie

225 g/8 oz plain flour · pinch of salt
1 teaspoon baking powder
50 g/2 oz lard · 50 g/2 oz margarine
65 g/2½ oz sugar · 65 g/2½ oz golden syrup
2–3 tablespoons milk

Sift the flour, salt and baking powder into a mixing bowl and rub in the lard and margarine. Add the sugar, syrup and enough milk to mix all the ingredients to a fairly stiff dough. Roll the dough out on a lightly floured surface to a large round, 5 mm–1 cm/¼–½ in thick and place this on a baking sheet. Bake in a moderately hot oven (200 C, 400 F, gas 6) for 30 minutes. Eat warm, split and buttered, with a little golden syrup spread on top.

Dark Moggie

4 tablespoons black treacle
50 g/2 oz lard · 50 g/2 oz margarine
1 teaspoon bicarbonate of soda
1 tablespoon milk · 275 g/10 oz plain flour
2 teaspoons ground ginger
½ teaspoon salt

Warm the treacle in a pan with the lard and margarine until the fats have melted. Whisk the bicarbonate of soda into the milk and add the mixture to the pan. Sift the flour, ginger and salt into a bowl and gradually add the treacle mixture, stirring all the ingredients well together. Pour into a greased, shallow 30 × 20-cm/12 × 8-in baking tin and bake the Moggie in a moderate oven (180 C, 350 F, gas 4) for 30–45 minutes.

Yorkshire Fat Rascals

225 g/8 oz self-raising flour
½ teaspoon salt
75 g/3 oz margarine
25 g/1 oz lard
25 g/1 oz caster sugar, plus a little extra for sprinkling
50 g/2 oz currants
2 tablespoons milk
1 tablespoon water (optional)

Set the oven at hot (220 C, 425 F, gas 7). Lightly grease a baking sheet.

Sift the flour and salt into a mixing bowl and rub in the margarine and lard. Add 25 g/1 oz sugar, the currants and the milk and mix all the ingredients to a firm dough, adding a little water if necessary.

Roll the dough out on a lightly floured board to 1 cm/½ in thick. Using a 6-cm/2½-in plain pastry cutter, cut out rounds and place these on the baking sheet, leaving space between them to spread. Bake them in the oven for 15–16 minutes, until set and golden, and leave them to cool slightly on a wire rack. Sprinkle the Rascals lightly with caster sugar and eat them warm with butter.

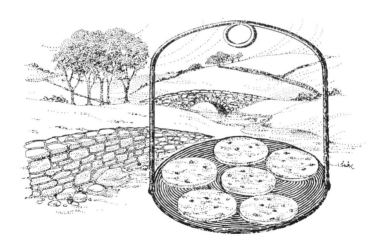

Almond Slices

Illustrated on page 104

Base
50 g/2 oz self-raising flour
50 g/2 oz plain flour
pinch of salt
50 g/2 oz margarine
1 egg yolk
2 teaspoons caster sugar
2 teaspoons water
apricot or raspberry jam for spreading
Topping
1 egg white
50 g/2 oz ground almonds
50 g/2 oz caster sugar
25 g/1 oz icing sugar
25 g/1 oz semolina
$\frac{1}{2}$ teaspoon almond essence
25 g/1 oz flaked almonds

Set the oven at moderately hot (200 C, 400 F, gas 6). Lightly grease a large baking sheet.

Sift the flours and salt into a mixing bowl and rub in the margarine. Beat the egg yolk in a small basin with the sugar, add the water and stir until the sugar has dissolved. Pour the mixture into the flour and fat, mix everything to a firm dough and divide the dough in half.

On a lightly floured surface, roll each piece of dough out to an 18 × 7.5-cm/7 × 3-in rectangle and trim the edges with a sharp knife and a ruler. Pinch up each of the long edges slightly to make a lip. Spread the rectangles with jam.

To make the topping, whisk the egg white until frothy but not firm and mix in the ground almonds, caster sugar, icing sugar, semolina and almond essence. Spread the topping over the jam and sprinkle it with flaked almonds. Bake in the oven for 25–30 minutes. Allow to cool on a wire tray, then cut each rectangle into seven 2.5 cm/1 in-wide slices.

Date and Orange Squares

225 g/8 oz chopped dates
grated rind and juice of 1 large orange
a little water
100 g/4 oz plain flour
175 g/6 oz rolled oats
100 g/4 oz soft brown sugar
175 g/6 oz margarine, melted

Set the oven at moderate (180C, 350F, gas 4). Grease a shallow, 18-cm/7-in square baking tin.

Cut the chopped dates as small as you can and put them into a pan with the grated orange rind. Make the orange juice up to 150 ml/¼ pint liquid with the water, pour this into the pan and stir the mixture over a low heat for several minutes, until it thickens. Allow to cool.

Mix together the flour, oats and sugar, add the melted margarine and stir the ingredients to a crumbly dough with a fork. Divide the dough in half. Press one half into the greased baking tin, spread the date and orange mixture on top and cover with the remaining half of dough. Press it down lightly and level the surface. Bake in the preheated oven for about 30 minutes, until lightly browned. Leave to cool in the tin and cut into 16 squares when cold.

Crunchy Biscuits

Illustrated on page 104

100 g/4 oz margarine, softened
50 g/2 oz soft brown sugar
1 tablespoon honey
25 g/1 oz glacé cherries
25 g/1 oz chocolate polka dots or plain dessert chocolate,
chopped small
100 g/4 oz plain flour

Set the oven at moderate (180 C, 350 F, gas 4). Lightly grease a
baking sheet.

Beat the margarine with the sugar and honey until fluffy.
Finely chop the glacé cherries and add them to the mixture
with the chocolate and flour. Mix everything well together
and drop teaspoonfuls of the mixture on to the baking sheet,
spacing them well apart to allow room to spread. Bake the
biscuits for 17–18 minutes, until set and golden.

Leave the biscuits on the baking sheet for 1–2 minutes,
then transfer them to a wire rack using a palette knife.

Index